i

By sipping a cocktail of short, thematically well-structured chapters, vignettes from practice, and personal creative dialogues, readers become part of an enthusiastic, collegial debate. The book combines rich content based on wisdom of experienced teachers with an easily accessible and systematic style. It presents theoretical concepts, which Gestalt therapists all over the world would use as a support for their daily work.

- Jan Roubal, M.D., PhD. Masaryk University in Brno. Co-editor of *Gestalt Therapy in Clinical Practice: From Psychopathology to the Aesthetics of Contact*.

As a unique and powerful form of Gestalt training, the Cape Cod Model has educated thousands about presence, power, intimacy, strategy, habits, resistance, trust, and change in relationships. This indispensable companion book is as near as you can get to grasping the spirit of the Model without actually taking part in it yourself. The key understandings, concepts, principles, values— even the "feel" —are vividly portrayed.

- Malcolm Parlett, PhD. Founding Editor of *British Gestalt Journal*. Author of *FUTURE SENSE: Five Explorations of Whole Intelligence for a World That's Waking Up*.

This book represents Gestalt therapy at its humanistic best. It merges a technique rich system with a quest for a streetwise understanding of the basics of living. It is difficult to be instructive while speaking with conversational familiarity but the authors pull off this challenge with vitality and wisdom.

- Erving Polster, PhD. Co-Author of *Gestalt Therapy Integrated* & Author of *Beyond Therapy*.

This book opened my eyes to a wider, quite practical, and not at all obvious perspective on human relations. Written in an elegant, clear, intimate, and at the same time, well-structured style, it makes good reading for anyone looking for practical tools to understand both intimate an social systems-and take action from a positive, optimistic perspective.

- Margherita Spagnuolo Lobb, Director, Istituto di Gestalt HCC, Italy

THE EVOLUTION OF THE CAPE COD MODEL

GESTALT CONVERSATIONS, THEORY, AND PRACTICE

JOSEPH MELNICK

SONIA MARCH NEVIS

A Personal Statement

This book is many things and results from years of immersion in the Gestalt world. It is not just about Gestalt therapy—but about a philosophy and way of life that has enriched both of us over our many years of working together and designing, along with others, the Cape Cod Model. We have had the opportunity to debate, collaborate, and hopefully contribute to the thinking and techniques that comprise Gestalt theory.

This book describes our relationship beginning in 1972, when Joe was first a student of Sonia's. We then became fellow explorers within the Gestalt world. In its essence, it is the result of what this journey has meant to us and how it has expanded our lives. After many years of teaching, laughing, theorizing and, in truth, learning together, we want to share with you what has mattered most to us.

We hope that by reading this manuscript you will be stimulated and find it useful in understanding our approach. But even more importantly, we hope that it will impact you in terms of how you live your lives.

To whom are we talking in this book? In fact, we are talking to nearly everyone, whether you are a therapist, organizational consultant, coach, or leader; or simply someone wanting to understand a little more about Gestalt and how it can influence life in a positive way.

As process-oriented practitioners and writers, we know that not every section of this book will speak to you. We hope that you will react and respond to some of the different elements (dialogue, vignettes, history, theory) and determine which bore you, challenge you, engage, and speak to you. For those of you experienced with the Gestalt approach, we wish for the book to reaffirm our core values and elegant theory. If Gestalt is relatively new to you, we hope that you will find encouragement to learn more and incorporate it into your work, practice, and above all, your lives.

This book is dedicated to the memory of
SONIA MARCH NEVIS, PhD
(July 10, 1927 – September 10, 2017)

Be generous; it's good for your heart.
Disappoint people with regret,
but *do* disappoint them.
Be curious; you'll learn continuously.
Talk directly to people, not about them to others.
Enjoy differences; we need others' perspectives.
Think optimistically, so that you see what's working.
Look for the humor in your life.

— Sonia March Nevis

ACKNOWLEDGMENTS

This book reflects the ideas of many. They include Bill Warner who, along with Sonia Nevis, created the seeds of the Cape Cod Training Program, and Joseph Zinker, who joined Sonia after Bill's untimely death. Later, Penny Backman, along with Joe, joined Sonia and Joseph and together were, for many years, the Cape Cod faculty. We were later joined by Carol Brockmon, Stuart Simon, and Sharona Halpern, who all made significant contributions to what has evolved into the Cape Cod Model. Nancy Rutkowski has recently become a part of the group. Until his death in 2011, Sonia's husband, Edwin Nevis, served as our sounding board, chief recruiter, and, head cheerleader.

Many colleagues read the manuscript through its various revisions. They include: Carol Brockmon, Kathy Curran, Donna Demuth, Susan Fischer, Tom Gross, Nancy Hardaway, Mark Koenigsberg, Jackie Sherman, Stuart Simon, and Zeynep Tozum.

Susan L. Fischer, editor of *Gestalt Review*, generously shared her expertise in helping to shape the book's final form. Desirae Page, Joe's long-time assistant, and Alysia Melnick, his daughter, put in many hours typing and re-typing revisions and his son-in-law Bob Smyth created the graphics and cover.

Gloria Melnick, Joe's wife, contributed her time and insights into creating the project. The book would have been much less if she hadn't volunteered her time as a copy editor and proofreader. Any awkwardness in the content rests solely on our shoulders. We are grateful for her ongoing support, both technical and emotional.

And finally, we acknowledge the contributions of the thousands of participants who have taken our programs and given us welcome feedback along the way. You have not only been our students, but our teachers as well.

CONTENTS

Section One.   **1**
History and Theory
1   Introduction   3
2   Origins   13
3   Intimacy   27
4   Optimism   51
5   The Cycle of Experience   63
6   How We Organize Ourselves   89
7   Creating Habits   99
8   Managing and Changing Habits   113

Section Two.   **127**
Expanding the Cape Cod Model to Larger Systems
9   Strategy / Intimacy   131
10   Power, Hierarchy, and Leadership   143

Section Three.   **165**
How We Teach Intervener Skills
11   Creating Trust   171
12   Intervention Skills   189

Section Four.   **221**
Putting It All Together
13   The Cape Cod Training Program   223
14   In Closing   247

Appendix A: Gestalt Core Concepts   253

Appendix B: A Sampling of Recent Books   259

Appendix C: Unfinished Business & Distortions   261

References   263

SECTION ONE

HISTORY AND THEORY

1

INTRODUCTION

This book focuses on a project that has been a major part of our professional lives over the past many years. We have written it to describe the *Cape Cod Model* (CCM), which we created and developed while teaching the Cape Cod Training Program (CCTP) at the Gestalt International Study Center (GISC). When we say *we created and developed,* we don't mean just the two of us. This book reflects the work of many—most importantly the CCTP faculty. In addition to us, Sonia and Joe, they included Joseph Zinker and Stephanie Backman, later, Carol Brockmon, Stuart Simon, and Sharona Halpern, and now Nancy Rutkowski.

We first began using the model with couples and families, then with teams and organizations, and most recently with consultants and leaders. What follows is not simply the description of a model, or merely a way of conceptualizing and organizing experience. It is a way of *living in the world*, a way of supporting psychological growth and of being more fully alive. What we mean by *living in the world* is a manner of embracing life, approaching others, processing what happens and moving on to our next experience. In our many conversations, we created a set of principles and values which, we believe, make for a good life. We have listed some of them below. These values and assumptions form much of the foundation of our model.

Before moving on, we would like you to take a moment to review them. Pay attention to which ones are clear, which ones vague, which you gravitate toward and which you pull away from, which feel profound and which seem trite. If you wish, you might show them to a friend and talk about them.

Underpinnings of the Cape Cod Model

- Awareness offers the opportunity to change. When something becomes a habit, we are no longer aware of what we are doing. For example, most of us are not aware of how we brush our teeth, drive our car, eat our soup, or talk to each other. When we become aware, we notice. Only when we notice do we have a choice between making a change, or doing things as we always have.
- Sometimes awareness can lead to depression and sadness, as when we become aware of pain, or we become aware of wants that cannot be fulfilled.
- Some of us pay attention to thoughts first and others first to emotions. To live well in the world, we have to be able to attend to both. Competency involves an ability to be in touch with both thoughts and emotions and being able to think *and* feel before acting.
- We all carry the past forever within us. The future—including our hopes, wishes, plans, fantasies, and daydreams—also exists. Yet we don't live in the past or the future as much as we would sometimes like. The *now* is all we really have.
- Every experience is composed of many ingredients that shift as a function of the moment and of the situation. It is the situation that is the primary organizer of experience, but most of the time it doesn't feel that way.
- Whenever two or more people are interacting—working together or talking to each other—whatever happens has been crafted by all involved. As simple as it sounds, it is a radical departure from how most of us understand our process.
- Every habit—whether good or bad—was used

4

initially to solve a problem. Most of our habits continue to be useful. Some, however, are no longer productive, but we continue to use them anyway. For example, many of us are taught to *be respectful,* more specifically, *not* to *interrupt when others are talking.* But if we always wait for a break in the conversation to speak, it might never happen. As a result, we might not express good thoughts or creative solutions that could help solve a problem. If we don't know how to speak up, how will people know what we know?

- The future is always unknown. We do not know what the next second, day, or year will bring. What we call spirituality is how we relate to the unknown. The unknown can scare, excite, confuse, or intimidate us. Some of us rely on hope and faith to support us in facing the uncertain future. We require a special form of competence to deal with the unknown. It consists primarily of the *courage* to sit with uncertainty.

- Resisting can be useful or useless. Competency involves knowing when to say *yes* and when to say *no.* This allows us to know when to act and when to wait, when to try new things and when to stick with the old.

- No one has ever awoken saying, "I am going to mess up my day." We don't plan on making mistakes, forgetting to make the important telephone call, talking too long with a boring person, denting our car, having a horrible meal, losing our keys, or yelling at our children. Most of us are doing the best we can, even when things don't work out as we had expected or hoped.

- Even the best of us messes up often. To turn against ourselves after we err is rarely useful. To experience competency is to know that these things are ordinary, and that the next day will bring new mishaps. And, every once in a while, we have a perfect day.

- Nobody owns the truth. There are many ways to look at phenomena, since we all see things differently. Competent behavior involves a willingness to talk and listen to other people who are different or who have different points of view.[1]
- Power is neither good nor bad, nor does it exist solely within individuals. Power exists *between* people, groups, and even nations. At its core, power is a relationship—not an attribute. A powerful person, group, or nation is skilled at influencing and open to being influenced. Some people are given power by their position, i.e., a parent or an employer, and they can use it for good or for ill.
- Most of our relationships contain some form of hierarchy, whether implied or explicit. In nearly all relationships there are differences in levels of knowledge or skill, and sometimes people are put in charge of others as leaders. Hierarchy needs to be acknowledged and respected, and the rules for clear communication understood by all. The health of a hierarchical system, such as a family or nation, depends on the relational competence of those in the hierarchy.
- We are always having impact, both good and bad, depending on how we present ourselves to others. We call our self-presentation *presence.* Becoming aware of our presence leads to acting with intention. Whether we are modeling a behavior, bringing a missing aspect to the process, choosing to remain silent, or joining with the group, we are always having an influence.
- Maturity, in part, involves creating lives that are filled

---

[1] There is much research that supports this notion. Even the legal system is questioning the validity of eye-witnesses.

with possibilities. We are able to move towards things that have potential, to feel regret when things don't turn out as expected, and to move on, having learned from the experience.

- And most important, growth and development come from our movement toward what is different from the way we are.[2]

Developing the Model

During our creative time, we did not imagine that we were developing something so coherent and organized as a *model.* As the years went by, the feedback we received indicated that our ideas had relevance far beyond anything we had ever intended. Participants in our programs told us that these concepts were, in fact, a philosophy for leading one's life. But our programs have always been more than concepts and philosophy.

We teach relational connecting skills, i.e., how to manage wants and desires, how to love and fight, how to create intimacy, how to hold on to what we care about, and how to let go gracefully and turn away when what we want and wish for is unattainable. These skills are applicable to various *levels of system*: individual, dyadic (lovers, friends, or work partners), group (family, project group, sports team, or therapy group), organization (corporation or religious group), or large system (political party or country).

Moving from Individuals to Systems

Let us say a little more about how we moved from working with individuals to larger systems. The Gestalt approach—helping people to live and function creatively in an ever-changing world—began with

---

[2] See Appendix A for a fuller description of Gestalt Core Concepts that are fundamental to the Cape Cod Model.

individuals. In the 1950s and 1960s, people flocked to Gestalt therapists, touched by the excitement of this *here and now* approach, wanting to learn and apply it to their lives. So, like most Gestalt therapists, we at the Gestalt Institute of Cleveland spent much of our time focusing on the individual. (See Chapter 2 for a description of our separation from the Gestalt Institute of Cleveland.) However, there came a time when we realized that working solely with individuals didn't allow us to reflect the true way people in the world interact, which is *with* other people. So, we began to develop a theory to describe how people interact together, focusing first on couples.

It was clear to us that couples, at least in the USA, were having trouble—fights, separations, and divorces—all stemming from failed relationships. It was baffling that people could get together with so much hope for the future and end up with the opposite—anger and conflict. We wanted to understand how couples could move from love to hate and from curiosity to disinterest, and we wanted to help them become more aware of themselves, their partners, and the two of them together. And last, we wanted to teach them to act and behave differently.

Buoyed by the success of our teachings, we became a bit grandiose. We thought that, if we could apply Gestalt principles to teaching couples how to interact, we could easily apply them to families, for they too had difficulty in relating and connecting. There we ran into a snag. The principles we used with couples were inadequate with families. In hindsight, the differences are both obvious and immense. Unlike couples, families are biologically hierarchical, and each member needs to manage multiple relationships. Addressing the challenge of families forced us to develop new thinking about power and hierarchy, and soon our theory expanded to include how to work with these concepts.

With more courage than we had before, we moved into the larger sphere of organizations. We were not surprised to find that organizations have many of the same sorts of hierarchical and power difficulties as families. But we also learned that there were many important differences. Once again, we were challenged to expand our theory and practice. We did, and we soon began receiving feedback that organizations were putting our approach to practical use around issues of leadership, hierarchy, and power—and that it was working.

Our Process

One problem with presenting a model is that it can be conceptualized as something linear like a map, as if it were developed in a structured way. It's easy to imagine a small circle of passionate people working through the night, sharing their ideas, testing out their concepts, and periodically responding with an *ah ha.* If only it were that easy! Looking back at our process, we find it was much less orderly. We talked with each other, we agreed and disagreed, we improvised, and we learned. The *model* emerged over time without much forethought as to what we were creating, and how it would all fit together. And this *we* are not just the faculty, i.e., those of us who have done the teaching and the writing over the years. The *we* includes the thousands of individuals who have participated in our training programs, in writers' workshops, in seminars, and in conferences.

Before proceeding, we would like to clarify what we mean when we say *how it developed* as opposed to *how we developed it.* We could also say *it developed us,* and also, *we developed each other.* All are true. We are the model. The model had as much to do with creating us, as we with creating it. This model—this creation—is a complex brew grounded in the Gestalt approach. All of us at the Gestalt International Study Center have taught it and expanded upon it. Students have influenced it. Our writings and conversations have shaped it. And the changing world has had an impact on it. This model is not an *it,* not a static entity. It has a life in that it is constantly changing and developing. Our guess is that, by the time you read this prologue, we will have added some new twists and components. And this ever-changing process is not only fine; it is as it should be.

This model developed often in a helter-skelter manner, with different pieces coming and going, as we explored our ideas with our students and with each other. These concepts were tested repeatedly, not just in the act of writing, but also in our teaching and in our intimate connections with each other. So, rather than flatten out our process so that it appears neat and organized, we want to present it as we lived it.

Overview of Book

This book has gone through many iterations, much like our model. Originally, it was to be a collection of our joint papers, tied together with some added prose; then an edited volume partially drawing on the ideas of others. Finally, we settled on the current format, a somewhat loosely structured collage created primarily from the writings and conversations between the two of us, as well as from what we have written alone and with others. We have also inserted vignettes and brief discussions we had as we explored the themes and concepts that eventually became the Cape Cod Model. We hope you find this format interesting.

As we take you along on our journey, we begin in *Section I* by discussing the Cape Cod Model's core concepts and operating principles. We then review the history of Gestalt therapy and also the Gestalt Institute of Cleveland (GIC). We believe that, for you to understand the model fully, you need to know where it came from. We also describe the creation and evolution of the Gestalt International Study Center (GISC) since this is where the model emerged, and since our Center still provides the platform for its ongoing growth and development. We then identify the basic challenges that face all of us who are trying to lead a relational life. We begin with *intimacy* because this has been our core interest as we have explored the nature of relationships. We follow with a discussion of *optimism*, which is an essential attribute of the Gestalt approach and specifically our Cape Cod Model. Following is a chapter on the *Cycle of Experience*, which describes the qualities of a good process, and we end the section by discussing *development* as a process of *pattern creation* and *destruction*. These are some of the major components of the original model.

Section II outlines the concepts we formulated and added when first working with families and then with organizations, including s*trategy/intimacy, power, hierarchy,* and *leadership.*

Section III presents a detailed discussion of *trust building* with a focus on *presence*, followed by *how to see systemically, how to intervene with impact by managing resistance, creating experiments, and ending well.*

Finally, *Section IV* describes our 16-day Cape Cod Model Training Program, so that you can see how we teach these concepts, and how we get them to live in the minds and hearts of our students.

2

ORIGINS

Gestalt Therapy

Our Gestalt journey and approach began in the 1950s and emerged in the 1960s and 1970s as one of the most powerful and popular of the humanistic psychotherapies. Our Cape Cod Model is rooted in Gestalt psychology and in the classic theory of Fritz Perls and Paul Goodman (1951). Because we focus on how we live in the world, the model continues to change and develop in relation to the different situations to which it is being applied. This makes sense. As situations change, so do we, and so do our relationships.[3] This adaptability of our process orientation to nearly every situation is what makes the Gestalt approach so powerful. For example, in the 1980s we began to apply our Cape Cod Model to organizations, since we were working with consultants, coaches, and leaders. (For a bibliography of recent books that address the Gestalt approach to larger systems and to interventions beyond traditional psychotherapy, see Appendix B.)

Historically, Gestalt therapy theoreticians and

---

[3] Our relationships involve sensations, actions, and gestures. They include our constructions of the past; especially unfinished and fixed situations and, of course, our anticipation of the future. This is what helps give our relational experiences form and shape. And by relationships, we don't just mean the individual, dyadic, cultural, sexual family of origin ones, but also the larger context that they are connected to, embedded in, and create, while simultaneously being created. See Robine (2015), Wollants (2012).

practitioners have rarely taught at universities. Few of the original Gestalt leaders felt comfortable there. Instead, the Gestalt approach flourished at institutes where the rules and structures were less reified. Our institutes created an anti-establishment culture that reflected Gestalt therapy's role as revolutionary within the psychotherapeutic movement. We did not publish much but relied instead on an oral teaching tradition to acquaint professionals with our theory.

We differed with most academicians in how we viewed theory development and research. Until recently, most academic research rested on a quantitative approach that was and is at odds with our phenomenological orientation—our focus on the uniqueness of human experience.[4] This focus has resulted in a vibrant, interactive, and lively Gestalt community. There are currently more than 400 Gestalt institutes around the world, numerous conferences and training programs, and an ever-increasing number of books being written and published focusing on Gestalt theory. However, our culture has bred a type of insularity, resulting in the Gestalt approach not generating much interest or impact in the *non-Gestalt* world.

The Gestalt Institute of Cleveland

Our primary founders were Fritz and Laura Perls and Paul Goodman, who were in turn psychiatrist, psychologist, and social critic and philosopher. In the

---

[4] There has been an increasing focus on research in the Gestalt community: the first international research conference was held at GISC in 2013, the second in 2015, and the third in Paris in 2016. A number of books have been published regarding research on the efficacy of the Gestalt approach. See, for example, Roubal, Brownell, Francesetti, J. Melnick, and Zeleskov-Djoric (Eds.) (2016).

1950s a group of psychotherapists in Cleveland heard about an amazing psychiatrist who had emigrated from Germany and South Africa and was then living in New York City. After watching Fritz Perls demonstrate his work, they invited him to Cleveland to teach.[5] Coming once a month for a number of years, Fritz captivated them. He was courageous and charismatic, and had a whole new way of looking at growth and development. He not only created a new form of therapy, but he also taught as no one had taught before. Sonia recalls the beginnings.

> **Sonia:** *I've been thinking about how I answer when somebody says to me, "What is Gestalt?" It happens often, and I think I answer differently each time. Is it about awareness, connection, contact, being present in the moment? I've never settled on a single response. Thinking about this question leads me back to my first experience with Fritz Perls. This experience bonded me to Gestalt therapy, to learning it, to articulating it so that I could teach it, to exploring its concepts in every which way.*
>
> *I had lived in Cleveland for a few years and then left to live in Chicago. When I returned, I found that my friends had heard about an interesting workshop in New York City that one of them had attended. It was about Gestalt therapy. They then invited the leader to give a workshop in Cleveland, and they were very excited about what they were learning. The leader's name was Fritz Perls.*
>
> *At that time, I had two daughters, a three-year-*

---

[5] The founders of the Gestalt Institute of Cleveland included Marjorie Creelman, Rainette Fantz, Isabelle Frederickson, Cynthia Harris, Elaine Kepner, Edwin and Sonia Nevis, Erving and Miriam Polster, Bill Warner, and Joseph Zinker.

old and a one-year-old, and had no thoughts about what I would do with the rest of my life. But I went to Fritz's next workshop, and my life suddenly had direction. That was over sixty years ago.

I have visual memories of that workshop, which are startlingly clear. I also have strong bodily memories of those few days that I can still call on to this day. I have almost no memories of the content of that workshop. What I know is that a fog had been lifted from me. Suddenly, I could see what was happening between myself and other people. I could name some of the feelings I was having. I realized that it was the first time I felt seen, and the first time I could see. Now here is where it gets hard. How do I articulate what I mean by such a statement? I think I have been struggling for a long time, as I am doing now, to articulate an experience that perhaps only poets should try to do. All I know is that the fog was lifting. From that time on my energy was focused.

We formed a study group from that workshop and helped each other grow. Fritz came back several times a year. Isadore From started coming in between Fritz's sessions. Then Paul Goodman, Laura Perls, Paul Weiss, and Elliot Shapiro also came. The nucleus of the Ohio Institute for Gestalt Therapy was formed in 1955.

Until the arrival of Perls, psychotherapy was a hidden profession, conducted behind closed doors. His stance was one of openness, rather than secrecy. Instead of lecturing, he would work live with volunteers and with the Cleveland psychotherapists. Rather than telling us what he did, we would watch and experience his work. He would develop it before our eyes—and with us. He would become interested in a concept and try things out with us. He valued learning, learning together, and he held the developing theory loosely, never being wedded to it. In fact, many of his ideas dropped out along the way when they were not supported by experience. Every time Fritz came to Cleveland he would say, "Forget what I told you last time—this is what is really important." He believed that theory should be close to experience, practical and useful. For Perls, theory and practice were always intertwined, each informing the other.

The faculty of the future Gestalt Institute of Cleveland (GIC) contained several individuals from the original group that first had brought Perls to Cleveland. They had different backgrounds, thoughts and ambitions, and they worked hard to manage their differences. Not only did they train together, but they also slowly became a community. They brought their families together to celebrate birthdays and holidays, and to mourn losses. During one period, many of them lived together in a housing community they created.

As its reputation as an outstanding training institute grew, GIC attracted an ever-increasing national and international enrollment. The faculty did more than train; they were active in theory development. And they, along with the next generation, also wrote, producing some of the most important books on the Gestalt approach (e.g., Clemmens [1997], Kepner [1987], Lee and Wheeler [1997], McConville [1995], E. Nevis (1987), E. Nevis, ed. [1992], Pappernow [1993], E. Polster and M. Polster [1973], Wheeler [1991], Wheeler and Backman, eds. (1994), Zinker [1977]) After completing their training, many participants returned home and started up their own institutes. In fact, it is estimated that around 50% of all Gestalt institutes around the world were started by GIC trained clinicians.

The GIC faculty was also drawn to novelty and to the expansion of traditional Gestalt theory. So, during a time when the primary focus of psychotherapy (Gestalt included) was on the individual, they stepped outside the norm, applying the Gestalt approach to couples, families, work groups, leaders, and organizations. And from the beginning, the faculty was also a learning community—inviting people with different and sometimes divergent views to join them and present their ideas to the staff.

Two of the founders of GIC, Bill Warner and Sonia Nevis, were fascinated by couples and families. Sonia's interest blossomed during the early 1960s when she taught couples therapy at Esalen Institute, where Fritz Perls was holding Gestalt residential training sessions. She understood intuitively our social nature. We are always in relationship to someone(s) or something(s). Bill, also a clinical psychologist, was a skilled family therapist, interested in the hierarchical differences between parents and children. Because of the mutual interest in each other's work, Sonia and Bill invited Carl Whitaker and Virginia Satir, two of the giants of family therapy, to teach and work with the GIC faculty for an extended period of time.

Whitaker, a wonderfully creative psychiatrist, understood the holistic and interdependent nature of relationships. Once, while in Cleveland, he interviewed a couple in therapy with a GIC faculty member and asked them to tell him something about themselves. The man described his life as a hard worker, while his wife talked about the many years she had spent in and out of mental health facilities. Without skipping a beat, Whitaker asked them how they had decided that she would be the crazy one. The man replied immediately, "Well, somebody had to work." Whitaker rarely practiced alone with families, always preferring instead to have a co-therapist. He believed in the value of relational connections—a value that we support.

Satir had a wonderful presence, a curiosity about

18

others, and loved engagement. In one of the GIC faculty's first experiences with her, she invited them to bring their families to a weekend workshop. She spent the first part of the workshop talking to each of the participants individually. A tall, larger-than-life woman whose energy could fill a room, she nearly had to lie flat on the floor to make eye contact with some of the younger children.

The relationship between Sonia, Bill, Carl, and Virginia grew and, in time, they began discussing the possibility of developing, if not an institute, then certainly a program that would incorporate many of their ideas. These dreams collapsed when Warner died while out jogging. It was 1979 and he was 51 years old. Satir and Whitaker eventually followed other interests and developed their own theories.

After a few years, Sonia invited Joseph Zinker to join her in her work with couples and families. Zinker, who by this time had written *The Creative Process in Gestalt Therapy* (1977), one of the most influential Gestalt therapy books, was known throughout the Gestalt world for his originality. Together Sonia and Joseph reconstructed the Couples and Family Training Program that became The Center for Intimate Systems and would eventually birth the Cape Cod Model. The original program was and still is taught in two eight-day sessions.

In recent years, GISC has added "The Cape Cod Training Program: The Third Week," which deals in more detail with the theory and practice of the Cape Cod Model; "Coaching and Consulting with Teams: Applying the Cape Cod Model in Organizations"; and an International Coaching Federation and GISC-approved coaching program, as well as numerous leadership programs, all based on principles of the Cape Cod Training Program.

In Cleveland, in the beginning, the participants were almost all clinicians, coming mostly from the USA. The original program contained a blend of lectures and experiences, consisting largely of role-plays and exercises. Because of the emphasis on experience, participants were invited to bring their partners and families for real life demonstrations towards the end of the program. The program emphasized *doing* over *talking about.* Therefore, the format included (and still includes) *live* demonstrations with *real* clients in front of the students, welcoming everyone's feedback, both positive and negative. In this way, the faculty never does anything less than is asked of participants.

As the program became increasingly popular, Sonia and Joseph invited Stephanie (Penny) Backman and Joe Melnick to join them. Penny is a highly experienced family therapist and, in addition to her Gestalt training, she had studied with Whitaker, the faculty of the Philadelphia Child Guidance Clinic, and many of the luminaries of the family therapy movement. Joe was originally an academically-oriented clinical psychologist, focusing his teaching and research on couples, groups, organizations, and social change. He trained with Isadore From, one of the founders of Gestalt therapy, as well as with the original faculty of the Gestalt Institute of Cleveland.

The four of us had known each other for many years prior to teaching together in Cleveland. Joseph (Zinker) and Sonia were senior members of GIC where Penny and Joe had originally trained before joining the professional staff and eventually the board. We then all migrated east for a variety of reasons. Sonia had moved to Cambridge with her husband, Edwin—considered by many to be the founder of Gestalt organizational consulting—when he accepted a position at the Sloan School of Management at the Massachusetts Institute of Technology (MIT). For many years, Sonia and Joseph had homes in Wellfleet, on Cape Cod. Joe had moved from Lexington, Kentucky, where he had taught at the university, to Portland, Maine, to live near the ocean; and Penny also moved there a few years later to establish a private practice and then bought a house in Wellfleet.

21

The four of us—Joseph, Sonia, Penny and Joe—were brought together not only by our Gestalt background, but also by our clinical interests, love of international travel, and passion for teaching, writing, and developing theory. We also enjoyed eating together and making each other laugh.[6]

**Joe Melnick, Joseph Zinker,
Sonia Nevis, Penny Backman**

Joe recalls his early connections to the Gestalt approach and how they expanded:

Joe: *During my second year of graduate school, I attended a sensitivity training (T-Group) weekend that changed my life. I couldn't believe what people*

---

[6] Eventually, we created the "Dim Sum Rule." We loved the experience of choosing and sharing food with each other, and would often meet in Boston to plan the program after having Dim Sum. As our Center grew and became recognized, colleagues began to approach us to join the faculty and teach in our programs. We decided that no matter how competent they were, if we didn't enjoy having a meal with them, they would be a bad fit.

were noticing and saying to each other. I became so enamored of this way of being and relating that I transferred to the University of Cincinnati, which had an emphasis on group therapy and process. I had a supervisor who was being trained at the Gestalt Institute of Cleveland and who would come back and tell me about ways of working with people that seemed magical. As a graduation present to myself, I signed up for an introductory weekend workshop at GIC. I had just landed a university position teaching group process and thought of myself as a talented group leader. My sense of expertise disappeared quickly, as I watched the leader work her magic. I still wasn't quite sure what Gestalt therapy was but I was hooked.

**Sharona Halpern, Carol Brockmon,
Stuart Simon, Joe Melnick, Sonia Nevis**

As the program changed and expanded, so did we. Carol Brockmon and Stuart Simon joined our faculty in

2005, and Zinker retired two years later. Carol, like Penny, is a highly skilled couples and family therapist; and Stuart, like Joe, straddles both the clinical and organizational world. Sharona Halpern, who combines her therapeutic interests with a focus on artistic expression, then joined our faculty; and Penny and Sonia retired.

The Sonia March Nevis and Edwin Nevis Meeting House, Wellfleet, Massachusetts (Home of Gestalt International Study Center)

We should mention a few more background factors that led to the creation of our own institute and the development of our model. For a long time, owning no physical space, we taught our program at different motels along Route 6, which runs the length of Cape Cod. The working space often left much to be desired. We still laugh about having to compete for airtime with a parrot that lived in one of the motels. In addition, since we all had moved east, we were feeling less connected to Cleveland and they to us. After much soul-searching, we decided to form our own institute and build our own

24

facility—the Sonia March Nevis and Edwin Nevis Meeting House—in Wellfleet, Massachusetts.

This friendly separation from GIC not only helped give us a new identity, but it also created openness to new people and new ideas. One should not underestimate the importance of having one's own home. Once we had a central place where we could gather, we had the time and place to sit with each other and develop the thoughts and ideas that eventually became the Cape Cod Model.

As mentioned earlier, although the two of us (as well as the entire faculty) started out as psychotherapists working with individuals, over the years we had learned that the original Gestalt principles could be expanded to function with more than one person. That knowledge supported us to develop more fully our work with couples, families, consultants, leaders, and organizations. Our discussions often focused on how to turn these Gestalt principles into good practice. We would talk, try out ideas, write, teach, and talk some more. Our collaboration always drew from our own experiences with each other, and from our friends, colleagues, families, and clients. It was always fun and creative. Throughout this process, the two of us, Sonia and Joe, would be in dialogue with each other. It was essential not to develop our ideas in isolation. Eventually, we would pick a topic (there were always many to choose from) and turn it into an article or book chapter.

Our collaboration resulted in two series of papers (from which we will be drawing throughout this book). The first was on relational development—how individuals, couples, families, peers, and work groups grow and mature. The second, growing out of our wanting to understand intimacy, focused on emotions such as surprise, desire, greed, jealousy, envy, disappointment, love, and contempt. We wanted to be able to look at all of these emotions, and especially intimacy, in a new way; a way that was less fixed, more fluid, and more related to how people respond to each other. Our work on intimacy and emotions is intertwined. It was essential for us to understand emotions, because emotional awareness is a precondition for relational connection and intimacy. And central to our writing has been the elusive concept of love, which for many is the desired precursor to intimacy.

3

INTIMACY

What Is Intimacy?

We are social beings. We grow and develop through connection, i.e., what Gestaltists call *contact*. One of the most sought-after forms of contact is intimacy: an elusive concept that conjures up powerful responses. Who isn't in favor of it? In fact, most of us readily admit yearning for it, and we tend to know it when we feel it. We can try to describe the sensations—a sense of oneness and connection—but how to create and maintain it is largely a mystery.

This *it* is something that seems to just *happen* to us, and the more we try to hold on to it, to bottle it up and preserve it, the more quickly it seems to slip through our fingers. We do know that there are certain experiences that elicit powerful emotions like joy and sorrow, sexual lust, and overwhelming despair; experiences that often set the stage for intimacy—at least of a short-term nature—to emerge. But understanding how to create, develop, and nurture intimacy in ourselves and others, this sense of joining and connecting during the humdrum moments of our everyday lives, is difficult indeed. Part of this difficulty is due to the fact that intimacy, as we said earlier, is hard to define:

> Some describe it as a closeness and depth between two individuals; an awareness of the innermost qualities of another. Others

27

emphasize reciprocity and an attitude of mutual permeability. Still others stress the sense of wholeness in the moment that can occur even between antagonists in a boxing match, for example. Lastly, some view it as a capacity or a characteristic that varies more or less among individuals. More recently, some have begun to emphasize the difference in capacities between men and women (Melnick and S. Nevis, 1998, pp. 39–40).

Intimacy, we have observed, is not defined by content, but by *relationship*:

Becoming intimate involves the process of going from an I to creating a we and incorporates a wish to know and a wish to be known. It is both a personal and interpersonal experience, a state of being with another, and includes thoughts, feelings and sensations. Most important, an intimate relationship is more than a transitory moment, it is a creative process, developed through repeated intimate experiences (Melnick and S. Nevis, 2006a, p. 29).

The operative word here is *process*, a perspective that is deeply embedded in the Gestalt approach:

By process we mean to describe the phenomenology of an encounter, emphasizing how experience is organized between two or more people. Thus, a Gestalt practitioner might be interested in specific characteristics or patterns such as complexity, robustness, liveliness, creativity, and balance to name a few. Because of its purely descriptive nature, a process approach allows us to avoid pejorative or judgmental constructs and language. For example, terms such as dependency or autonomy are ultimately contextual and refer to a certain aspect within a system (Melnick and S. Nevis, 1998, p. 40).

Part of the difficulty in arriving at a consensus regarding the meaning of intimacy lies embedded in the powerful feelings, images, and archetypes that it evokes. Although we may disagree regarding a precise definition, we somehow seem to know it when we experience or see it. For example, when we think about intimacy, we can easily call up images of a mother nursing her newborn child, two lovers walking hand in hand along a deserted stretch of beach, two elderly companions gently rocking side by side, or three friends absorbed in a discussion.

Intimate Moments

Because intimacy means so many different things to different people, we believe that it is important to differentiate short-term intimacy, what we call *an intimate moment,* from long-term intimacy. Intimate moments can occur quickly, seemingly without much work, and disappear just as suddenly. We can experience that fast and powerful sense of connection with another (e.g., what we sometimes call *infatuation),* or in a group (e.g., when people mourn the death of a good friend, or celebrate the victory of a sports team together). Because of the ease with which they are created, intimate moments, that sense of profound connection and loss of boundaries, often mask their elusive and short-term nature and often convey a false promise when confused with long-term intimacy. This confusion can lead to much embarrassment, pain, and suffering.

There are potential opportunities for intimate moments that go unnoticed every day. It is the noticing and entering into these relational experiences that provides the lubricant for connection, whether with another, a couple, a team, or an organization. And the connected moments provide the fuel for a relational life.

Long-Term Intimacy

It is our belief that the most important requirement for the development of long-term intimacy in couples is that it occurs between equals. This means that there exists between intimate individuals a system of mutual and balanced caring and concern. Ultimately, the survival and growth of any long-term relationship rests on a genuine relinquishing of one's need to be more or less powerful than the other and a deep understanding that individual resources belong equally to the couple's system (Melnick and S. Nevis, 1998, 44–45).

For intimacy to develop within a couple, time must be spent living in the ordinary—sitting side by side, holding hands and watching television, cooking a meal together, or talking things over as you drift off to sleep. Then there are the memorable moments, the ones that stand out, the ones that the poets describe. And by memorable we don't just mean the joyous ones; we also mean times when a loved one is sick, a job is lost, or there is a death in the family. But even more is necessary for intimacy to develop and thrive. We need to be able to move from who is right or wrong to an interest in what is going on between us. We have to learn to bear and work through betrayal and disappointment, to confront broken promises—both our partner's and our own—and to forgive hurtful words and thoughtless actions. These are the experiences that make for a long relationship that is rich, exciting and, above all, never the same.

Joe: *A few weeks ago, I saw a couple in my office for the first time. He is a physician, and she a lawyer; they have three small children. The wife said to her husband, "If it wasn't for the kids, I'd be out of this marriage. You never listen to me."*

Sonia: *It sounds like they have no time for each other. If you don't have time, you can't listen, you can't connect. People jump over this point. They seem to keep trying to move ahead but never appreciate the full cost of not enough time. Our whole way of living is characterized by not enough time.*

Joe: *I like what you're saying, because intimacy is usually slow-moving.*

Sonia: *Yes,* slow *is lost in our culture. The quick pace wasn't as true twenty-five years ago. I think that we should put in some support for slowing down. Our culture focuses primarily on one element, on the action. We settle for thin contact. We don't stop and say, "This is not good." We don't really look at our own behavior. We take quick action as normal.*

Joe: *Can we get back to the couple? I was hoping that this woman wouldn't say it, but she finally did. "I love you, but I'm not in love with you."*

Sonia: *What happened next?*

Joe: *He seemed sad, but not surprised. She had stopped their sexual relationship a year before, because she wasn't "in love." He wasn't happy, but he seemed to have accepted it.*

Sonia: *In my practice, I have a couple that can't stop interrupting each other. They know that they need to pause, but they can't do it yet. Both of them need to say everything in the*

31

moment. They can't sit back and listen. They are not paying any attention to what is being said to them. They don't stop to say, "Do you understand what I'm saying?" They rush, rush, rush, and then they don't understand why they don't feel connected.

Joe: *Yes, people will speak and not notice the response, that is, what is happening to the other person.*

Sonia: *I think I am talking about something a little different. If you said, "I love you," I think I would also say "I love you" rather than saying, "Thanks." Most conversations involve my saying something, and your saying something slightly different. So, I am teaching people to say, "Do you like what I just said?" There is a different feeling tone, and it takes twice as much time. But that is what is being thrown away.*

(Here we shift to role-play. This has always been one of the ways we work together, creating an experience that is partially our clients, partially us.)

Joe: *Suppose I said "I love you."*

Sonia: *I might say, "I'm glad you told me."*

Joe: *My response would be, "What do you love about me?"*

Sonia: *"You're a pain in the neck." I don't want to break my love into pieces.*

Joe: *I like my persistence. You don't like it?*

Sonia: *Why do you need to go and get something from me? What for?*

Joe: *I want to know how my words impact you.*

Sonia: *I told you. You're a pain in the neck. It sounds a little bit like you want to squeeze things out of me rather than be curious as to what will*

32

come from me. You could say, "I wish you would say more things to me."

Joe: Suppose I said "When I come home at night, I wish you would stop reading the newspaper when I walk in and be less critical of me. That's what I want."

Sonia: I want to be able to give you what I want to give. I don't want to be told what I should give, or what I should say. I'm different from you. I don't want to pick up my head when I read the paper. I might say, "Hold it, I need to finish." But anything that you do to push me to stop would not work.

Joe: I don't want to push you. I want you to be excited when I get home.

Sonia: I'm not that type of person. Go find someone who will give you that. But you're not being very nice to me. You're being critical of all the things that I don't do. You miss these things?

Joe: Yes, you used to look forward to seeing me, and now you don't.

Sonia: But you're telling me that I'm not good enough.

(Out of role-play)

Sonia: In reality, I don't like it when people are pushing me to do things. It's not two of us together.

Joe: Let's get back to the couple. She actually said, "I don't think you listen to me."

(Resuming the role-play)

Sonia: And I would say, "Yes, so what do you want me to do? You keep implying that I'm a bad person, because I am not doing it the way *you want me to do it. So, what is it that you want from me right now? I'm willing to hear it."*

Joe: *I want to understand why I don't feel connected.*

Sonia: *I'm hearing that you want certain things from me that I don't understand. Tell me something that you want me to do.*

Joe: *I want you to understand. I want you to hear that my heart is shut down.*

Sonia: *I understand that you are feeling some pain. Have you told me that before?*

Joe: *I did for a while, and then I stopped trying. You just don't get me.*

Sonia: *Hey hey. . . what is "getting you?"*

Joe: *Empathizing with me, putting yourself in my shoes.*

Sonia: *All you are doing is telling me what made it bad on my side. I believe I need to ask you a lot of questions. I think I must have done that at one time. I understand I don't say, "I'm glad you're here." But I need to hear more. I am willing, but I don't know what to give.*

(End of role-play)

Joe: *Many couples want magic, like it was at the beginning.*

Sonia: *They want something, but they can't quite tell each other what it is.*

Joe: *Yes, and they can blame each other, or they can say that the feeling is gone, and they want to find it elsewhere.*

Sonia: *When couples come together, no matter how aligned they are, they don't know what each other is thinking. The only way to work things out is for each to ask.*

Joe: *That's the curiosity that often dies. When couples are infatuated, they don't have to ask.*

Sonia: *Often in infatuation, even if I don't want it, I still take what's offered. I think of early times in my marriage. Why didn't Edwin (her late husband) ask me if I wanted a drink? He was going to give me what he wanted to give me. I have in my drawer tons of jewelry that I didn't want. I didn't say in a nice way, "I don't want a drink, or I don't like that type of jewelry." And he would have learned to ask. So, the whole thing about being able to ask and get an answer is the key to a good relationship. Do you agree?*

Joe: *Yes. Most clients don't know what's going on with their partners. Not because they are stupid; they just can't know. So, back to the client who says, "You don't get me." It is true. You can't know.*

Sonia: *They have to say, "What is in the way of your asking me?"*

Joe: *People who really come together in that first stage of wonderment don't realize that they don't know the first thing about the other person. You never know what's inside them.*

Sonia: *It is difficult to accept the notion that we are all so different and that trying to make the person into the one we want them to be is a fool's errand. After romantic love ebbs, we realize that we didn't get what we thought we were going to get. And people get angry because they feel ripped off.*

How does intimacy develop?

At the beginning of a relationship, much of the

couple's focus is on one another. As a result, a great deal of everyday life is often ignored. However, as the relationship develops over time, there is generally less to be discovered about the other. This wearing off of newness is often perceived as a great loss, and to some extent it is. However, the increased familiarity also brings with it some positive benefits. There is often a transition from learning about the other to learning about the relationship. Furthermore, much of the interest and energy that originally went into discovery becomes available for daily living. At its best, a type of balance ensues in which personal, relational, and wider needs get appropriate attention (Melnick and S. Nevis, 2003, p. 230).

Originally, we called ourselves The Center for the Study of Intimate Systems. We did not choose this name casually. We worried about whether the word *intimate* would generate sexual associations and images rather than enhancing people's understanding as to what intimacy is really about. But after much thought we decided to keep the word, because intimacy is what most people crave.

All of us need to know how to make connections on many different levels, to see and be seen, to speak and to listen, to touch and be touched; in sum, to be in relationship. Learning how to experience the back and forth flow of connection, which seems so natural when we are in early relationship, is difficult and requires an array of skills. In fact, we have witnessed over and over again people's surprise when they realize how much work it takes not only to grow a relationship, but just to keep it alive. But most of the time it is worth it. Maybe it is simply that there is something inherently profound in knowing and being known. To be seen, understood,

36

and acknowledged touches the core of what it is to be human. It is as if we are designed to be in relationship with another, without goals or agendas. Many have written about this experience, but few as eloquently as Martin Buber (1937).

There is, however, also a downside to this increased knowing of the other. What is familiar, complex, and predictable can quickly become uninteresting and boring. Aspects and characteristics originally experienced as attractive and novel can unexpectedly take on a more negative hue and become problematic, defying resolution. Let us present a vignette of a developing relationship:

> *Like many couples, John and Mary became attracted to each other because of their differences. John loved Mary's spontaneity and playfulness; she loved his passion for work. As the relationship grew, they began to experience the downside of this originally attractive polarity. Mary began to notice that John had difficulty relaxing, and that work took him away from her. She found herself competing for his time. Rather than relaxed and playful, she was becoming resentful and tense. John, on the other hand, originally attracted to Mary's energy, began to notice that Mary never seemed to get things done. She was, to his surprise,* irresponsible. *He began to resent the burden of planning their lives.*

This vignette ends at a crucial point for Mary and John. For their marriage to succeed, they will need to learn to manage their relationship creatively. For example, they will need to learn to deal with the surprise and disappointment that comes with discovering that, as time passes, what was originally attractive starts to fade and often even begins to repel us. This learning is not easy. Nor is the next step, learning to develop the *good form* to manage these disappointments.

Being with another complicates our lives at every moment, and not always in good ways. Once in relationship you have to give up a good deal. So why not be alone? There are many reasons, but most important is the huge satisfaction we get from giving support to and receiving support from each other. This allows us to face the world in a sturdier way.

Intimacy Skills

Intimacy develops over time as we experience and work through many different relational situations. When we told our students that intimacy involved being able to begin, move through, and end experiences well (see chapter 5 on The Cycle of Experience), they said that they believed us but needed more. If one can learn specific skills in order to cook, play chess or the piano, and even make love, why couldn't we teach students skills so that they could be better at creating intimacy, not only in their own personal relationships, but also with their clients, patients, and employees? We took them seriously and over time, this is what we created.

(1) Learning to manage differences

After people are together for a while, they begin to notice differences. One is better at some things; one is better at others. One likes to get up early; one likes to sleep late. For their relationship to develop, they need to understand that we all experience things in our own manner, and we need to learn to manage differences in creative ways. In fact, one of our core beliefs is that *growth and change come from embracing differences.*

(2) Keeping interest alive

Staying interested requires an ability to notice when boredom or caricaturing has set in, and to engage and be engaging. Over time, both sharp disappointments and a gradual diminishing of interest in the other need to be addressed. To paraphrase Perls et al. (1951), the couple's *novelty* naturally lessens:

> As the relationship field becomes more and more familiar, energy for the other is more difficult to generate. The couple is left with a dilemma to resolve. They must learn to mutually create a process that is ongoing and unending, that infuses the relationship with vitality and positive newness, while at the same time develop habits and patterns that allow them to move freely about in other parts of their lives. Ultimately, they will have to find a rhythm that supports them in creatively adjusting to the relationship (Melnick and S. Nevis, 2003, p. 231).

(3) Using humor to contribute to the softening of interactions

We view humor as perhaps the most important skill needed for intimacy. It serves to balance the hard work and discipline, the disappointments, hurts, broken promises, disillusions, and betrayals. It allows us to soften the pain and disequilibrium that always occur in relationships.

By humor, we do not mean that we see these feelings and experiences as "funny," or that humor should be used as a deflection from reality. Humor allows the intimate couple to move to the larger awareness of all human frailties and frustrations and to smile at them. It combines negative and positive emotions at the same time, and therefore supports our expression of negative feelings without being stuck. It allows each of us to stay in contact with the other, when moments of conflict and anger have the potential to shatter the *we* and lead to withdrawal.

Ultimately humor allows conflict to be safe, for it is a way of modulating energy and arousal. It is a way of letting off steam. In intimate relationships, humor allows the couple to take themselves less seriously. It lifts the weight, for embedded in it is support of the *we*. Humor, when used sensitively and respectfully, provides a short cut from the negative to the positive. It allows us to move on. Sonia describes a relevant exercise:

Sonia: *We have done a group exercise in which a couple first does a task together. Then they split up and each does it with someone other than their own life partner. Once again, they split and do it with a third person. It never fails that they start out very earnestly and very seriously with their own partner. When they go to the next person, there's a lot of laughter in the room and again much laughter when they go on to the next person. When they go back to their own partner, they become very earnest, conservative, and serious once more. It is the same pattern every time.*

For us, there is little doubt that laughter is an essential ingredient for successful relationships. It leads us to *ask* ourselves the following questions: *What is the role of earnestness and seriousness? And what is the role of playfulness, joy, laughter, and fun?*

In the beginning, before a relationship is a committed one, play is in the foreground and earnestness is in the background. Then, when it becomes committed, it switches over to earnestness

40

with some play. And then, at a certain place in life when it's appropriate for earnestness to diminish, a successful relationship can switch back to play as foreground. Those may be the relationships that are envied by other people who see them. Those are the long-term ones that people want to emulate. It's not that they've been playful all along—they're playful, then earnest, then playful again. (E. Nevis, S. Nevis, and Zinker, 1986, p. 1).

(4) Being willing to influence and be influenced

For relationships to develop, both parties must have the ability to put themselves forward and impact the other; to say what they want and do not want. They need to do it in a respectful way that allows for discussion. Similarly, each partner must be open to being impacted and to hearing different opinions; to be able to sit back and ask questions.

> **Joe:** *A couple came to me because they were having difficulty being heard. Both are successful executives who know how to persuade and how to make a point. As they began to realize that they were all about "output," and that they had lost much of their mutual curiosity, they began asking questions, taking a breath before responding, and so developing the "we" in their relationship.*

(5) Bearing disappointment and disappointing others

> Disappointment seldom exists in a beginning relationship. At the start, what is new and different is rarely unsatisfactory. In fact, most novelty is pleasant and discoveries are usually positive and welcomed. However, as

relationships mature and positive projections decline over time, disappointments naturally occur. They must be viewed as normal and ordinary, not as a sign that the relationship is in trouble (Melnick and S. Nevis, 2003, pp. 235-236).

We often ask our students to notice whether they are more comfortable disappointing someone or bearing disappointment. We also ask them to notice at which of these skills they are better. They often find that they are good at one of these behaviors and poor at the other.

(6) Creating good form

Each creative process has a structure. In the arts, people are trained technically and aesthetically to know *good form.* Potters, for example, are taught to perfect their artistic sense while mastering the skill of working at the wheel. Couples (and work teams), on the other hand, are seldom taught the concept of good relational form. Usually their knowledge and skill base derive from a blend of unaware and unexamined "shoulds" and "should nots" handed down from their parents and the wider culture. We once put it this way:

> If this is the case, then how do we assess good form, especially since there are no designated experts or critics other than therapists to evaluate the product? It is hard enough to assess a good piece of art or a musical performance, even with some agreed upon criteria, but how do we determine a successful intimate relationship? (Melnick and S. Nevis, 2003, pp. 227–228).

Our concept of good form involves the Cycle of Experience, which we discuss at length in chapter 5. It allows us to look at experience as *wholes* or what we term *units of work*. Thus, good form consists of an ability to connect at the beginning, to do the task, and to end in a good way.

(7) Focusing on the here and now

Intimacy is dependent on living in the here and now, connecting through what is present in the moment, be it a joyful or sad experience, or an interaction of agreement or dispute. This is not always easy, because we all carry traces of our past hurts, joys, and disappointments into each present moment. Sometimes the impact of the past can be high, especially if we are unaware of it. Bringing the past *effectively* into the relational present is an important skill. There is a difference between, "You did this and didn't do that," and "Remember when we took long walks together and struggled to learn to talk to each other?" It is the focusing on the here and now that is the cornerstone of Gestalt therapy and the Cape Cod Model. For even when we are fantasizing about the future, the present is still where life occurs (E. Polster, and M. Polster, 1973).

(8) Having the capacity to work hard and the discipline to live out agreements

At the beginning of intimate relationships, relating is not hard. There is something about the early days that is naively sweet. We often don't appreciate how thin our connection really is. When time begins to challenge that ungrounded sense of connectedness (intimate moments), people are always stunned. We have to appreciate that hard work is necessary for the relationship to grow, and then decide if it is worth it. As we said:

> For most, new relationships just seem to happen without much effort. In fact, if one had to work hard in the beginning, most relationships would never develop. Few infatuated couples can ever imagine all that it will take to maintain and nurture the connection. Not surprisingly, some believe that if intimately relating to someone takes so much hard work, there must be something wrong. (Melnick and S. Nevis, 2003, pp. 233–234)[7]

(9) Creating novelty throughout: Having an experimental attitude and methodology

We proceed here with citations from our writings.

> The creative couple must be committed and willing to take the risk, break the rules, let go of old forms, and be willing to fail: in essence, to destabilize. How do they find the courage to do this? It involves practicing a major component of the experimental attitude, the ability to let go of outcomes and—even more importantly—to let go of critical judgment. (Melnick and S. Nevis, 2003, pp. 234–235)

> An experimental attitude involves a willingness to interrupt or transform one's ongoing life temporarily in order to *see* or perceive the other and the relationship in a new and different way.

---

[7] This common idea, that the creative process is a spontaneous, easy event flies in the face of research on creativity and creative individuals.

It is driven by the question, "What would happen if. . . ?" and is based on a commitment to try out new forms without critiquing or evaluating them immediately. By this we mean that the couple does not have a heavy investment or interest in viewing the relationship through the lens of success/failure. Instead, each displays a willingness to explore the other's perspective. Rather than being interested in outcomes from the stance of good/bad, the focus is on what is learned from the experience. An experimental attitude embraces the unknown and accepts the uncertainty of change. In order to translate these experimental values and beliefs into living, the couple must have a methodology for creating novelty within the relationship. This methodology helps to define the shape and the form of the unique creative process. For example, they have to discover how much change and newness is enough, and thus how much is too little or too much. (Melnick and S. Nevis, 2003, pp. 232–233)

There is a sense in which we can view long-term relationships as works of art. Suppose you purchase a beautiful painting. Over time as the newness fades, it is easy to lose interest and succumb to being dulled and desensitized by it. For many, buying a new painting fills the need for novelty. But with an experimental attitude, even the most predictable of patterns contains novelty and generates many creative options. For example, we can stay longer looking at the painting. We can look at it in different and fresh ways to capture the subtle nuances of the work. We can discuss it with others, asking their impressions. We can move its location, change the lighting, or group it with other paintings. Can we recover the feeling we had when we first saw and desired it? Probably not, for the first time comes only once. *What we can do, however, is create novelty by expanding the ground and shifting our relationship with it.*

Turning back to the couple, "an experimental attitude and methodology incorporates a commitment and ability to look with freshness at old patterns, no matter how functional and effective they are. It further involves the skills to let go and change these patterns in order to remain involved in a process of continuous discovery of new ways of experiencing the self, the other, and the relationship" (Melnick and S. Nevis, 2003, pp. 232–233).

(10) Finding the right blend of autonomy and connectedness

Although we value self-support, we also advocate embracing dependence as a value to be acknowledged and toward which we should move. Intimacy includes the willingness to give up autonomy and to experience neediness. At the beginning, the Gestalt approach overemphasized self-support and independence—the ability to rely on oneself to move forward in the world. That was the original definition of a mature adult. It led to the popular Gestalt Prayer by Fritz Perls that begins with, "I do my thing and you do your thing," and ends with "and if by chance we find each other, it's beautiful. If not, it can't be helped."[8] But self-support at the

---

[8] "I do my thing and you do your thing.
I am not in this world to live up to your expectations,
And you are not in this world to live up to mine.
You are you, and I am I,
and if by chance we find each other, it's beautiful.
If not, it can't be helped." (F. Perls, 1969, p. 4)

extreme creates a shell around the individual and minimizes dependency and vulnerability—the ability to be impacted profoundly by an intimate other. It reduces the ability to feel pain, loss, and sorrow, but also joy and happiness, as we have indicated elsewhere:

> What of maturity as self-support? Independence and self-support are necessary when no intimate other exists for dependence and support. Dependence and awareness of the other are necessary for relatedness with an intimate other. In a true intimate relationship, both individuals have the capacity to aesthetically blend the poles of the autonomy-dependency continuum. (Melnick and S. Nevis, 1998, pp. 50–51)

(11) Co-creating experience

Every relationship and every situation are unique. There are no bystanders in relationships. Even when one seems to have made a *unilateral* decision, both have been a part of it, no matter how large or small their perceived roles. Every moment together is co-created, and both have some responsibility regarding the quality of the created experience. It is this inability to own one's part in the co-creation of experience that often leads to the refrains "I should have known better," "Why didn't I listen to my gut?" or "How could I have believed him again?" The acknowledgment of co-creation minimizes *blame*, an onerous emotion which is unfortunately all too present in many relationships.

(12) Knowing when enough is enough, when to hold on, and when to let go

In order for a couple to generate novelty, they must be skilled at letting go of old forms. This process is called *creative destabilization.* Sometimes this is easy—the old forms just do not work. For example, neither one enjoys going to concerts anymore. But what if the old forms still have some life in them? When is the right time to let go of the familiar, so that the novel can emerge? When are we hanging on a little too long? The creative couple must have the ability to break paradigms and repetitive patterns, promote unusual expectations, and thus create fluidity, flexibility, originality, and novelty.

This is rarely easy and often feels entirely undesirable. There are many legitimate reasons to hold on to stability and to embrace the practical and familiar. What if the new is less satisfying than the old, and we end up rejecting what is valuable along with what is useless? We all have within us a fear of the unknown. Yet, it is just this holding on stance forged from our fears that stifles creativity.

In Closing

So, what is intimacy? You may have noticed that we have not used the word *love,* for it is even harder to define. For some, intimacy conjures up sexual passion. In fact, many think of it only as that, but in truth it is many things; most of all *a joining experience*, a sense of connection. And, of course, intimacy can occur not just within couples, but also between fans at an exciting game or a fabulous concert when there is heightened energy, and in an organization in which a work team that has been struggling *suddenly* begins to click together. We call these experiences *intimate moments,* for the sense of connection usually comes and goes quickly. However, most of us strive for long-term intimacy. Unlike intimate moments, that is not something that seems to happen *to* us but something we create together. To do this requires a set of beliefs and a set of skills.

Our primary belief is that nearly everything that goes on in an intimate relationship is co-created; each is responsible for the good and the bad. Righteousness and keeping score never work. Last, as we discuss in the next chapter, an intimate relationship requires an optimistic perspective, an ability to take what comes while being open to the other and to experience. And of all the skills we need, we favor humor and playfulness most of all. We value an ability to not take ourselves too seriously, to see the absurdity of so much of life, and to be able to gently laugh at ourselves, our intimate others, and our relationships.

We developed the Cape Cod Model to create a process that can lead people to have a *connection*; to learn which parts of this complicated joining process they do well, and which parts they can improve. Helping couples, teams, and organizations to grow requires special skills on the part of the helper. This is what we teach in our training program.

We involve our students in many relational experiences as intervening partners, in which they work with couples, families, groups, and leadership teams— some simulated, and some real and long-term. And we have them be clients, as well as leadership and work team members. Relating to different people, different situations, and different parts of themselves—*with support and awareness and without judgment*— maximizes learning.

4

OPTIMISM[9]

We are born with an ability to reach out and explore the unknown and engage the future with curiosity. This ability, if nurtured, results in a forward leaning, an open and interested orientation that we call an *optimistic perspective* or *optimism*. Although there are many benefits to this perspective, most importantly it allows us to meet the uncertainty of the next moment with the energy to deal with whatever emerges. However, we are also born with the polar tendency, that of *pessimism*. Rather than being expansive, a pessimistic perspective is narrowing. It is tense rather than relaxed, fearful rather than courageous, backward as opposed to forward-leaning. Of course, both orientations are necessary, and have their appropriate places in our lives. Given the seemingly unsolvable conflicts that exist in the world today, anyone who has an exclusively optimistic stance is, at best, naïve.

Sonia: *I think most people go first to the negative, and they do it easily.*

Joe: *Yes. I know that's my natural tendency. But I'm not sure why.*

Sonia: *It feels safer. People don't want to be told what is wrong by someone else, or to have to wonder what criticism might be on the other's mind—a kind of unspoken wrongness. So, to avoid being hurt or disappointed by another's comments, we often go immediately to* what's

---

[9] A version of this chapter appeared in *Gestalt Review*, 21.3 (2017), pp. 191–199.

wrong *and express it first.*

Joe: *Yes, I remember a friend at school, Ed, an excellent student. After every exam, he would come over and tell me how miserably he had done. Of course, he would always get A's, and no matter how hard I tried, I couldn't get him to see what he was doing.*

Sonia: *Yes, he was protecting himself.*

Joe: *And the price he paid for the protection was the loss of an opportunity to feel good—or at least not bad. If I let myself feel good, I am more vulnerable. Then if bad things happen, it's a longer way to fall.*

Sonia: *Remember when you were teaching at the university, and you would get class evaluations?*

Joe: *Yes, I'd always jump over the good ones and search for the bad ones.*

Sonia: *Well, I went the other way. I found a way to focus on what's good.*

Joe: *I've always seen you like that.*

Sonia: *When I was growing up, I never had someone tell me what was right or wrong. No one ever asked me what I thought. I could have gone in the opposite direction. I could have thought that everything was awful. I've never thought about what it is like to have someone waiting for you to do it right.*

Joe: *Someone in your situation could have had an awful life.*

Sonia: *Yes. I don't know why I didn't. Maybe it's because I also had nobody who said, "Stop—don't do that." I lived in five different homes the year after my mother died in childbirth. I was five years old. Optimism is often used in the wrong way—as if we know what will happen in the future.*

52

Joe: *What do you believe makes people optimists?*

Sonia: *I think of it as my willing to try things when I don't know what will happen. I dive into the pool because I want to know what will happen. I don't think about whether it will be good or bad. I think, "Why not?"*

Joe: *Yes, optimism isn't a belief that something good will happen, for it will or will not. It's not about a guess concerning the future.*

Sonia: *Optimism is about having the courage to try things. It's about stepping into something because we hope it will be a good thing, without knowing what will happen.*

Joe: *And it's also about learning not to stay attached to the negative when things don't turn out in ways we had hoped.*

Optimism/Pessimism

There is a lot of discussion as to whether we are hardwired for optimism or for pessimism. The proponents of optimistic wiring point to our overly optimistic predictions of the future and our ability to put a positive slant on the past. But others argue that our bodies are configured more for pessimism; that we are designed to respond to sudden changes such as physical danger with a reflexive fight or flight response.[10] Then, after responding, we rest. This "fight or flight response" worked well when most danger was life-threatening and only intermittent. But danger is different today; it is mainly psychological and is often ongoing. But our brain does not differentiate between physical and psychological danger such as when the stock market dips, we struggle with alcohol, we get a

---

[10] "For women it is often not 'fight or flight,' but 'tend and befriend,' due to higher levels of oxytocin in their bodies" (Curran, 2015).

53

poor performance review, or our spouses seem to be losing interest in us. When we are feeling in danger— real or imagined—our internal wiring is for *fight or flight, quick arousal,* and then rest.[11] But how do you *rest in between* when you think that your business might go bankrupt, or your husband might be having an affair? Like our brains, our bodies also do not experience a difference between physical and psychological danger, nor do we know how to manage continuous stress.[12]

Unfortunately, this fight or flight design is ill-suited to contemporary times, for in our lives today we must deal continuously with an unending bombardment of stimulation and environmental changes. Even on a global level, war and disease appear constant. It seems that whenever one conflict or disease diminishes, another quickly takes its place. Simply said, no longer is there respite from stress. We seldom experience a sense of deep safety as the pace of our lives continues to increase, and words such as *multi-task, overwhelmed* and *stressed out* describe the usual. As a result, our world, as it exists internally, with others, or globally, has become more and more complex and unpredictable. Chaos is the norm and no longer the exception. In sum, postmodern life produces very few natural resting places where we can relax.

Our task is to learn to live well in these times. As we have said, we believe it requires an optimistic perspective, one that supports our bearing the uncertainty of life instead of automatically responding to unexpected situations with a fight or flight response. Learning not to focus immediately on what is potentially

---

[11] For an excellent summary of the biology of fight or flight and the brain, we recommend Strossel (2013).

[12] One of the hallmarks of the diagnosis of Post-Traumatic Stress Disorder is a heightened and continuous state of physiological arousal, even when there is no apparent physical danger.

dangerous, or potentially wrong, is essential. For that ingrained search for what is wrong leads us to the reflexive fight or flight response.[13]

Changing this pattern of pessimism is not easy, because we come from a culture and an educational system imbued with the belief that, if you show people all that they do wrong, they will grow and develop. But the truth is often just the opposite. When you tell people what they do wrong, their interest in development diminishes. On the other hand, *when people become aware of what they do well, they and their relationships grow.* Optimism is fundamental to much of what we are talking about in this book. It stems from the Gestalt principle that *all of us are doing the best we can, given our assessment of the environment.*

Paul Goodman said that the only way to manage evil is to turn prisons into hotels and treat those severely damaged people well. He would place them on an island with basic amenities. He understood that they could not live in society, but he also believed that when we embrace an eye-for-an-eye approach to living, it creates an unending cycle of pain and violence. Contempt breeds more contempt and resentment (Melnick and S. Nevis, 2010). Sadism and punishment, although understandable responses to violence and abuse, seldom work in the long run.

The people who come to us for help are usually lacking in an optimistic perspective. They have tried to

---

[13] There are many excellent programs and approaches that focus on dealing with trauma. A few of them are Somatic Experiencing®, founded by Peter Levine (1997); Developmental Somatic Psychotherapy, created by Ruella Frank (2001); and Stress Reduction Clinic and the Center for Mindfulness in Medicine, Health Care, and Society, created by Jon Kabat-Zinn (1994).

change and solve their problems but haven't succeeded. Most of the time they know where they have fallen short, caused pain, failed to act, or behaved carelessly. Many overvalue the *what* and the *why*. To join them in gaining another *insight* into why and how they have failed might seem useful in the moment but rarely helps.

Optimism is at the core of the Cape Cod Model and, in fact, of Gestalt therapy itself. It is important to remember that the Gestalt approach was born in the 1950s and blossomed in the 1960s as part of the humanistic movement (see Fisher, 2017a, b, c). *It rests on a belief that history is not destiny and that just one powerful experience can be enough to change our lives.*

Optimism and Pessimism Defined
- *As character.* Historically, optimism and pessimism were viewed by psychologists as part of what we call *character* or *personality*. This *sense of identity* is necessary for providing a type of psychological continuity as we move from situation to situation. However, if this sense of identity remains the same and is not impacted by the current situation, the individual's growth and responsivity are limited— creating what we term a *fixed Gestalt.*
- *As traits.* Optimism and pessimism were seen as *traits*, as basically unchangeable, with some of us more naturally one or the other as we engaged with our world. Although this scenario is still somewhat true, it has been found that we have far more control and influence over these tendencies than many have believed in the past (Achor, 2010).
- *As habits.* Optimism and pessimism were seen as habits of thinking, as explanatory styles; i.e., how we explain the causes of bad or good events (Seligman, 1991). The defining characteristic of pessimism is the belief that bad events will last a long time.

Pessimism is connected to helplessness and an inability to affect what happens to you. Pessimists believe that they are primarily responsible for their pain and suffering. They give up more easily, are depressed more, tend to ruminate, and are unable to move to action, movement, and change. In sum, they appear stuck. Optimists on the other hand experience life as more random. They have less anxiety, stress, and sickness, and are more creative and open to new ideas. Optimists literally have a broader vision and *see more.*

- *As orientations to the future.* Optimism and pessimism are ways of dealing with the ever-present unknown. Should we buy the lottery ticket or not, take a new job or stay with the old one?
- *As attitudes.* Optimism allows us to put our energy and effort into helping to create a *good next moment*; one that represents what we wish for ourselves, our intimate others, and the world. This is the type of energy we put into a desired future. It means working for what we want to happen—working, not just wishing.
- *As ways to live well with uncertainty.* Ambiguity is a fact of life; the only thing we know for sure is the present. Optimistic people know how to live with uncertainty. They know how to embrace it and not be a victim of it.
- *As ways to understand the past.* By identifying one's previous inclination toward optimism or pessimism, one can better understand the choices made and the feelings experienced in the past. When people come to us, they are often stuck in the past and filled with self-blame. They are surprised when we tell them that it serves no purpose to blame themselves or others, unless their purpose is to feel bad. We say, "The time when feeling bad would have been useful was before you acted. Feeling bad now won't

help. What you can do is learn from this experience, because every experience has both positive and negative aspects." What often surprises them most is when we tell them that no matter how bad things are, there is almost always some good embedded in it; of course, the reverse is also true.

> **Joe:** *Some years ago, I received a phone call from a friend, Vince, telling me that our close friend, Stuart, had died during the night. I had just spoken to Stuart a few days earlier, and he had seemed fine. The three of us were old friends from graduate school and had been getting together once or twice a year for many years. We talked about how horrible Stuart's sudden death was, especially since life lately had been going well for him. He had just resurrected his career as a senior organizational consultant and was doing exciting and challenging work. "Yes," I said, "at least he died at the top of his game." "But," Vince said, "remember that the better he did, the more he worried?" He then remarked about how sad it was that Stuart would never see the completion of the beautiful house he had been renovating for years in Northern California. I started laughing when I realized that Stuart also would never again have to deal with the ongoing anguish of the unfinished house. This good news/bad news rhythm continued as we found ourselves alternating between laughing and crying.*

- *As a perspective.* Optimism and pessimism are ways of seeing and understanding experience. In our training program, we sometimes ask participants to pair up and to think of an upcoming event in which they do not know the outcome. We ask them to take turns describing it twice: once from a positive, and once from a negative, perspective. The listener's task is to pay attention to the body language of the speaker. When we ask the listeners what they noticed, they usually talk about how the speaker, when relaying the event from a negative viewpoint, seemed low energy and somewhat collapsed. On the other hand, when the speakers described the same event from a positive perspective, they seemed animated, lively, and energetic.

Insight and Optimism

Most psychotherapies value *insight,* a sudden understanding that connects current behavior to the why's, how's and who's of the past. We believe that learning how to create the conditions for insights to occur is one of the primary goals of practitioners of the Cape Cod Model; and that these conditions involve an understanding and ability to see and restructure patterns.

By this we mean that an insight is simply a reorganization of experience. Learning to see differently is what opens us up to new possibilities. Being able to take something we are confused about, can't seem to make sense of, or habitually brings us pain, and then to stand it on its head so that it *makes new sense*, is what creating insight is all about. This can only be done with an optimistic stance, one that leads to becoming friendly with confusion and old habits, instead of wishing to avoid or destroy them. And it is this new habit of accessing insight that allows us to let go of, and add to, the old. But to give up our old beliefs takes trust and openness to new experience. The sense of *ah ha,* so connected to insights, is both a result of being open to experience and the creator of new ones.

Outcomes of an Optimistic Orientation

- Optimism creates *positive energy.* As energy gets generated and expands, possibilities emerge. We notice many more things and are able to experiment. When we are energetic, we are able to look at what is worth doing and what is worth trying. There is much research suggesting that if you are moving and not stuck, you are healthier, both physically and emotionally (e.g., Seligman, 1991).
- Optimism leads to *curiosity.* Being interested is the antidote to some troublesome interpersonal habits such as *stereotyping* and *caricaturing,* which bind energy and keep relationships frozen and narrow (Melnick and S. Nevis, 2010).
- Optimism leads to *asking questions and being creative.* It is knowing the difference between a guess and a belief. It moves the process ahead, allowing us to try new things and generates the capacity to deal with whatever life hands us.
- Optimism leads to *success and achievement.* "It turns out that our brains are literally hardwired to perform at their best not when they are negative or even neutral, but when they are positive" (Achor, 2010, p. 4).
- Optimism leads to *hope.* This allows us to articulate wants and creates visions for the future, keeping many from despair and depression. "Have you ever bought a lottery ticket and imagined what you would do with the money if you won? You knew it was a fantasy, but the small *ray of hope* propelled you into a sweet illusion" (Melnick and S. Nevis, 2005, p. 20).
- Optimism leads to *courage.* Courage transforms hope into action. Hope needs to be wed to realism,

or it is not enough. Courage is more concrete and more focused. It allows us to turn fantasy and the energy of hope into doing. Courageous individuals can generate the energy to act and to live out their hopes as they enter the world of the unknown.

- Optimism gives us the *strength to fail*. The truth is that most creative lives are filled with failures. We all know about losing, but optimists are resilient and more comfortable with the disorganization that failure brings. They are able to learn from experience and move on. Optimists embrace failure, because they know that we don't learn unless we are able to risk. A life without many regrets is a life narrowly lived. Sonia recalls a life example:

> **Sonia:** *One of the things I regretted in my life is that I never had taken music lessons. As an adult, I decided to take some piano lessons, and I looked around for a teacher. The first few teachers I approached told me that they didn't like to teach adults—only children, because adults can't bear to make mistakes and children don't care if they mess up. Anyone who has ever tried to learn an instrument knows that, in the beginning, almost all you are doing is making mistakes. As a result, teaching adults is not fruitful because they drop out quickly. I finally did find a teacher I liked, and who never shamed me when I failed. So, failing became quite ordinary for me, and I learned to accept it.*

- Optimism can be learned and maintained. We talk about this notion in the rest of this book.

In Closing

Optimism allows us to help create our wish for the future. Sometimes our work pays off; sometimes it doesn't. Optimism allows us to accept what happens, even if it doesn't turn out the way we want. It allows us to celebrate, mourn, and then to move on.

Many turn away from seeing the world through optimistic eyes because they, like all of us, have been disappointed many times and feel cheated and betrayed. So, they turn their back on optimism and say, "That is ridiculous." Since they want to avoid the *sensation of disappointment*, they turn away and connect with all the things that don't work well. *It takes courage to be optimistic, while knowing that we fail more than we succeed.* And there is no question about this. Many people have said that you learn most through failures, but we disagree with that idea.

We still hope for success, even though we know that we will err again and again. Optimism gives us energy not to linger in the bad moment too long. Optimism, even in the midst of failure, allows us to move on to the next moment and leads us to a willingness to try again.

5

THE CYCLE OF EXPERIENCE

Joe: *The Cycle of Experience (Cycle) seems so fundamental to how we organize and live our lives. In truth, experience is more a wave function than a cycle, for there is never a true completion of an experience, whether a meeting, a marriage, or a life. Endings always create beginning. Although inaccurate, we use the term "cycle" because it is easy to grasp, despite its seeming oversimplification of experience.*

Sonia: *Yes, I can remember when we at GIC first started creating the Cycle a long time ago. We used it as a way of informing people about what they were doing. People seemed to take in the image. It seems so simple. When you start something, you have to know how much time you have and how much space you have in terms of what you want to get accomplished, and then you have to put it all together. You have to act and then you have to finish on time. There is something important in knowing that you are always in flux.*

Joe: *What appeals to me and it seems simple yet profound —is that every full experience has a beginning, middle, and end. We all have our own preferences as to which parts of the Cycle we like best. I know I've always hated endings. I like middles.*

Sonia: *I think that it is the same for me. I also hate endings. I'm not particularly in love with*

63

beginnings either. The beginning and the ends are slow.

Joe: *I've always found beginnings a little awkward. I want to get into the meat of things quickly.*

Sonia: *I first realized the value of the Cycle when I began working as a therapist. I had an hour. I always ended on time, no matter what. I never went over. And that orientation came out of the Cycle. I knew when I needed to end. Now it is in me. It's about beginnings, too. It doesn't matter whether it is 15 minutes, an hour, or a year. I remember when I would teach, I would take a breath and look around. By that time, the students are ready to hear and for me to speak. I take a little time to orient.*

Joe: *I recall working with a group of litigators and teaching them the Cycle. As a profession, they tend to be action-oriented. They are still impressed with the value of starting their meetings with a brief, relational check-in.*

Sonia: *Yes. We first started talking about our individual Cycle. And now we are talking about a Cycle for a group or organization, and what we see is that they often don't know how to organize time and energy—that there isn't a sense of a beginning or an ending. They go straight across. Nothing has ended and nothing has started.*

Joe: *Yes, we can learn a lot about people as individuals, couples, teams, or organizations by what they emphasize and de-emphasize in the Cycle.*

Prior to the Creation of the Cycle

In looking back to the 1950s when the Gestalt approach began to rise in popularity, psychologists were legally prevented from doing psychotherapy. They were also excluded from psychoanalytic institutes, which taught the primary therapeutic modality of the time. They functioned principally as testers, researchers, and teachers. However, as more and more psychologists were trained and supported by programs created by the United States Veteran's Administration, they became more interested in the therapeutic enterprise. This was when, for example, the group in Cleveland began meeting (see Chapter 2) and eventually became acquainted with the Perls, Hefferline, and Goodman groundbreaking book, *Gestalt Therapy: Excitement and Growth in the Human Personality* (1951). Utilizing this book as their primary guide, they struggled to find a way to translate this theory of psychotherapy into something that people could use in their ordinary lives.

Up until that time psychotherapists aspired to be a *blank screen,* removed from the therapeutic experience, thus allowing their patients to *project* their experiences onto them. The goal, as we have said, was *insight*; an intellectual understanding of how past experience (primarily childhood) had helped shape the individual and contributed to his/her internal dynamics. Therapists did not overtly express their personal beliefs, opinions, and feelings, but instead worked hard to keep them hidden. Despite their best efforts, they were not always successful (see Melnick, 2003).

> **Joe:** *A colleague of mine told me of his first visit to a psychoanalyst. Prior to walking into the waiting room, he went to the men's room to relieve himself. He glanced at the man at the next urinal, but neither said a word. He then took a seat in the waiting room.*

When the analyst called his name, my colleague became aware that this was the same man that he had casually encountered in the bathroom. The analyst took a breath and explained that he would have to refer my colleague to another analyst because the therapy "had been contaminated."

This belief in the importance of imposed distance and minimal responsiveness began to change as the humanistic therapy movement swept the field. One of the most important of these psychotherapies was that of Carl Rogers who replaced the term patient with client, and believed in the importance of empathy, connection, and respect as the cornerstones of an effective therapeutic experience. Although we valued the humanistic perspectives of Rogers and others, we felt that they did not go far enough. While appreciating the importance of empathy, connection, and respect, the Gestalt approach, specifically as expressed in the Cycle, also valued action and learning by doing. Our approach freed the therapist to experiment and to say, "Try this."

Sonia: *As I began to develop as a therapist, I started saying to certain clients, "I am going to take off my therapeutic hat and tell you what you could do and try." Several years later, I was asked to be on a panel of psychologists. They brought in a keynote person who had had a lifetime of therapy. This man asked the group, "Do you want to know who the best therapist I ever had was?" He went on: "The last one; a man who said, 'Cut your hair. Go to a good tailor and get yourself a well-made suit.'" His therapist understood that all the many insights were not helpful until the young man knew how to use them for everyday living.*

The Creation of the Cycle of Experience

The founders of The Gestalt Institute of Cleveland created a visual template for describing the flow of experience and named it the Cycle of Experience. Originally drawn as a circle and taken from the work of Perls, Hefferline, and Goodman (1951), it described an individual's internal experience:

> The Cycle of Experience summarizes the process by which people individually or collectively become aware of what is going on at a given moment, and how they mobilize energy to take some action that allows them to deal constructively with a new awareness. It defines a unit of work and involves the experience of knowing something, of making meaning and assimilating. (E. Nevis, 1987, p. 1)

The Cycle was often talked about in biological terms, such as eating. For instance, you feel tension in your stomach *(sensation)*, then focus on your belly and notice that you are hungry *(awareness)*. You begin to become interested in food *(mobilization)* and move towards the refrigerator *(action)*, where you select an apple. You then eat it *(contact)* and after your appetite is satiated, you reflect upon the experience *(meaning making)*, move to an open stance *(closure)*, and soon begin a new cycle. Over the years the Cycle has been changed in many ways in order to make it understandable and useful. And this process of change and revision will undoubtedly continue, for any theory about relationships cannot be stagnant. The elements that currently go into the Cycle of Experience are described briefly below (see *Figure 1*).

- **Sensation**

Traditionally, sensations were viewed as the beginning of experience. We are always experiencing sensations, for the brain never goes to sleep. At the core of sensation is movement, constant movement throughout our bodies. Life is continuously filled with sensations: changes in light, temperature, different voices, the wind moving, or the birds singing. We are always surrounded by and immersed in them.

One of the important tasks necessary for a full rich life is an ability to manage our sensations. At any specific moment, we have to heighten and develop some of them, while the rest stay in the background, whether for a moment or a year. Most of the time, we do this automatically. We tune out the tick of the clock, the tension in our back and the noise outside our window.

There are no words or labels attached to pure sensation. For example, the sensation of a heartbeat is pure. We could objectively describe it, for instance, in terms of the number of beats per minute. But putting meaning on it is a whole other story. It could represent an upset stomach, the beginnings of a heart attack, or something more psychological—anticipation, dread, or something else.

Yet there are sensations that are often ignored because they are connected to old, often traumatic experiences that we have learned to avoid. For example, many who have been sexually abused have avoided not only sexual sensations, but also people of power because both call up traumatic associations. Imagine what it is like being abused and unable to do anything about it. This past inability might continue to keep us feeling powerless and often sexually confused in the present.

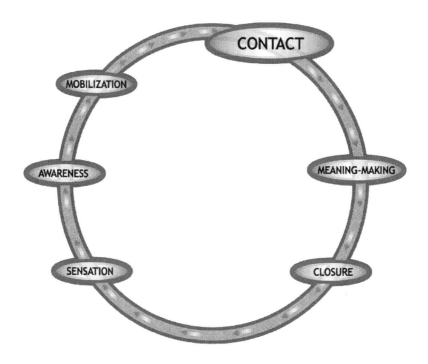

Figure 1: The Cycle of Experience

For many of us, our ability to move on is connected to becoming aware of these old sights, smells, tastes, and kinesthetic experiences that are hard to bear. When some of these sensations are brought into awareness with enough support, it allows us to be more courageous, to manage the powerlessness arising from the early trauma, and to create new possibilities for living in the world.

> **Joe:** *A client came in for a relationship problem. Women took advantage of him. As he spoke, he clenched his jaw and smiled. As he talked about his childhood, he recalled his experiences in parochial school with a series of nuns who would punish him for any behavior, no matter how mild, that they viewed as deviant. In his previous therapy, he had*

connected his inability to hold his ground with women to these experiences; yet he still continued to make bad choices.

As he began focusing on his smile and clenched jaw—"Clench it more. Smile more," I said—he became aware of the anger and aggression he had learned to contain at an early age. As he clenched and loosened, smiled and frowned, he started to sit up straighter in his chair. He understood that, as a child, he had made a good decision—not to speak out and challenge the nuns even when they were unfair and sometimes sadistic. But he also began to understand the cost of continuing this behavior as an adult. He realized that he had other options.

It should be noted that, historically, we viewed sensations originating from the body in a somewhat simplistic way. Modern research shows that the brain is not just the responder but often the activator of sensations. For example, there are many research-based programs that teach people not to be activated around pain (Kabat-Zinn, 1994). Instead, they can learn to focus on other things that interest them rather than on their sensations, so that the pain will recede. Focusing on other things is one of the many ways for us to gain control over these difficult sensations.

- **Awareness**

Much of our lives involves moving from moment to moment without much awareness of our self, others, and our surround. And for much of the time we can live a good life without much awareness. For example, some of our lives are lived via *intuition,* like a mother breast feeding her infant, or a parent soothing a sick child. And sometimes we act with only minimal awareness, such as in an emergency. Yet awareness is essential in order to grow, develop, and behave with options and possibilities.

Becoming aware is an awakening; an awakening that is often energizing. When we identify, categorize, or name sensations (for example, when we label our sweating and rapid heartbeat as either dread or anticipation), we are able to move towards what we want or away from what we don't want.

Awareness is the cornerstone of both the Gestalt approach and the Cape Cod Model.[14] It is the ability to be aware that is essential for a well-lived life. We are not just talking about general awareness. *Competency involves an ability to choose the awareness that has current relevance and possibilities; the ones that we can do something about.* As we indicated previously, to be aware constantly of chronic pain seldom serves a useful purpose.[15]

Originally the Gestalt approach focused on being aware of sensations. It emerged as a counterbalance during a time when the Western world paid attention to *thinking, acting, and doing.* To be aware is an Eastern perspective, one that focuses on being in the moment rather than doing and achieving goals.

Let us turn briefly to the topic of awareness in

---

[14] The concept of awareness, often under the label of "mindfulness," has become integrated into many contemporary therapeutic approaches.

[15] There was a time when our beliefs around dealing with trauma were quite different from how they are now. Therapists believed that heightening painful sensations, bringing them into awareness, and expressing them was a way to control the pain. Unfortunately, it often doesn't work and, in fact, sometimes will increase the pain. Instead, we now understand that focusing on something else (as Kabat-Zinn does in his chronic pain programs) can actually make the pain recede. The brain does the work. See also Taylor (2013).

relational development. Infants do not have a well-developed awareness of others, beyond their being a resource for meeting biological and emotional needs. As a result, children have to be taught such basic skills as sharing, making up, compromising, and collaborating. As we become socialized, our awareness of self-expands to include significant others in a different, more complex way. Ideally, we learn to have a well-developed sense of who the other is, and care about him/her in a lively, yet bounded way. And as we explain later, we learn to *carry* not only others within us but also our *relationship* to them and their relationships to significant others. But these types of awareness of the other, though necessary, are still not enough. For full development to occur, we must learn to be aware of when and how our actions will affect others and their actions us.

As awareness of the other develops, it expands beyond the confines of physical presence. For example, we all have experienced the sense of violation that occurs when someone we care about has not considered us in our absence. This *lack of awareness of the other* often results in painful experiences, reflected in common phrases such as: "Why didn't you call?" "How come you didn't ask me?" "Why didn't you think of me?" "Didn't you know that I wouldn't like it?" (Melnick and S. Nevis, 2006a, pp. 30-31).

> **Joe:** *When I was a graduate student I was taking a required class in statistics. There was a man who sat in the front of the room and dominated the class with his questions. Many of us became annoyed with him and would make fun of him behind his back. One day, I confronted him about his poor class manners. To my surprise, he first looked stunned and then said, embarrassed, "Why didn't anyone say something to me?"*

Just to be aware will not give us the balanced life for which we yearn. As the Cape Cod Model developed, we began to understand that being able to stay in a state of fluid awareness is often not enough. We also need to have the skills to mobilize and move towards what is novel and different.

- **Mobilization**

To reiterate, as we experience our sensations, we become aware and energy builds. Mobilizing is about energy, the psychic drive that is basic to living and keeps us moving through life. As we become interested, our awareness becomes heightened and focused, resulting in a signal to us about what is important in the moment. As we mobilize, our awareness sharpens and all the other potential interests recede into the background. Our interest and emotional energy begins to grow, ultimately organizing a want, a desire (Melnick and S. Nevis, 1995). In response, we either move toward something or away from it.[16] Said simply, the task of this phase is to form a sharply delineated figure out of a rich and varied background.

- **Action**

Acting is the last stage in which energy rises. As we experience ourselves as coming closer to wanting to act, possibilities continue to narrow. One might say that we are experiencing *intentionality.* It is important to note that we are moving toward or away from someone or something. Action that is not grounded in awareness

---

[16] Of course, another option is to do neither—to stay frozen and not act while the energy increases. Unfortunately, this mode results in panic attacks, phobias, and the general stress and anxiety that many psychotherapists spend their days addressing.

can be problematic. We often call these behaviors impulsive. We've all had the regretful experience of acting hastily, looking back shaking our head, and wondering "Why didn't I think first?" Premature action can lead to feelings of being out of control.

Joe: *When we look at two people moving through the cycle, the process becomes much more complex (we will discuss this further in the next section). More time needs to be spent on the awareness stage than when there is just one person; being aware of what is going on inside oneself while simultaneously trying to stay connected with others is not easy. To join well, we have to be aware of all our wants. And then building on this awareness, we must have the courage to move toward others—to act, to speak, to gesture, to touch, i.e., to find a way to act on our joint wants.*

Sonia: *Yes, in time we diminish our awareness, and we act without thinking or feeling much, and this is often good. Obvious examples are becoming proficient playing an instrument or in speaking a language. After a while, these skills become automatic, but sometimes these unaware actions can be extremely destructive. For example, alcoholics can describe how they can go to a party, promising themselves that they will enjoy the conversation and avoid having a drink. Yet ten minutes later, they can find themselves having had three without having experienced a choice.*

Joe: *Let's get back to action as a form of connecting. As humans, our primary form of connecting is speaking, yet we often speak* *without being aware of our thoughts and emotions, not to mention the person to whom we are speaking. Speaking is an example of an action that can be performed either with awareness or outside our consciousness. In truth, we seldom are aware of why we speak.*

Some of the reasons are presented in the citation below:

Does this seem like a strange thing to have to figure out? This is because many of us don't realize that there are many types of conversations. Knowing when to speak and when not to speak involves not only having a developed sense of others, but also of context and timing; not just the how of speaking, but also the why— the intentionality behind the words. We speak when we cannot self-soothe ourselves out of disappointment and we wish others to join us. We speak out of curiosity—to hear our words aloud or to wonder what the other will say. Sometimes we speak so as not to be alone. We speak to say new things, to change old habits. We speak to give feedback, to increase awareness. For example:

➤ Do we differ in terms of goals? What do you hope to get out of the talk? Is it to figure out who will pay for the groceries? Do you want support in landing a job? Do you want to apologize or to express your joy?
➤ Are you speaking to give me some information; to convince me of something? Are you speaking to connect with me?
➤ Are you speaking because you are lonely and don't want to be alone right now? Are you speaking because it hurts too much to remain quiet?
➤ What do you want back from me? Do you just want

to be heard? Do you want information? Do you want to reach a decision?

Before starting an intimate conversation, you have to ask yourself the most important question: Are you in a place where you are open to hearing what I have to say? Why do we not speak? We don't speak because we are reluctant to be a nag, to repeatedly confront the same issue, are hesitant to escalate or hurt the other, or because the other is emotionally unavailable at this time (Melnick and S. Nevis, 2006a, p. 35).

- **Contact**

Contact was originally thought of as an *all or none* experience. As illustrated in Figure 1 above, contact followed action and was in turn followed by meaning making and closure. You were either *in contact* or *not*. Now we view it as existing throughout the entire Cycle. The form (its direction and intensity) changes based on the amount of energy expended.

Contact is a relational concept. It traditionally means *being invested in seeing and being seen, hearing and being heard.* If I want to make contact with someone, I need to make sure that I am reaching them and also have to be open to being impacted myself. Initially, contact was viewed as a *touching of the other at the boundary.* By touching, we of course mean more than physical. We can touch with our minds and hearts, not just our bodies.

Sonia: *The first time I heard of the concept I was puzzled as to how it could help me. At a workshop one of my teachers gave me an exercise. I was asked to face another at a distance, and the two of us were asked to begin walking slowly toward each other and to pay attention to the point when our body said to us, "This is as close as I want to get." We*

76

both stopped at the same time, knowing that we had come to a place where we were connected. We knew the truth of contact in that moment.

- **Meaning Making**

When we work with our clients we watch for the amount of energy put into the different stages throughout the contacting process. Ideally, there should be less energy in awareness, since awareness is just the beginning of knowing what we want. Energy increases as we mobilize and move toward or away from something. As we move through life we are always in a biological cycle of sensation, awareness, mobilization, action, and contact. But there is one more stage after action, *meaning making*, where the energy diminishes in order for new awareness to emerge.

At some point after we have acted and engaged, we begin to turn away, to lose interest. We are saturated, feeling satisfied, disappointed, or often both. We have done what we need to do, and we have started naturally moving towards an ending. We are becoming less energized as we begin to let go and make sense of what just happened. We turn to thinking, considering, and evaluating the experience, and deciding whether we liked it or not.

This stage is marked by a return to ourselves as we integrate the learning, appreciating what has been, and regretting what could not be. This is a slow stage because most of our interest in the experience has waned, and we are now letting go, withdrawing, and moving towards closure. Common examples of meaning making may be found in critiquing a movie with a good friend, striving to understand how our family could have gotten into such a painful argument, or celebrating a successful project launch. In organizational as well as in therapeutic work, bringing the work to an end is often minimized and sometimes ignored totally. For example, many meetings end abruptly without the participants describing what they took from the experience—what they learned and liked, and what they wish to do differently next time. Sometimes the reverse is true. Meaning making can occur prematurely, short circuiting the process and thereby potentially drowning out experience. And sometimes it can result in a stereotyped search for causes that keeps us wedded to the past.

> **Sonia:** *I have collected glass figurines in my office for many years, all shapes and sizes. Sometimes when I am ending therapy with patients who struggle with that moment, I will ask them to select a figurine and break it. They are often surprised and may physically pull back. They will sometimes say, "Don't you care about it?" I might answer, "Yes, very much." They will say, "So why do you want me to break it?" I'll say because the sensation of loss is one that most of us avoid, even though it is so ordinary. We all have to learn to experience it in the moment. If we are lucky, we can do it with another.*

- **Closure**

If we have successfully moved through the Cycle, the learning from our experience has become background, moving out of our active awareness. We become open to the next moment. And so, we are ready to move on.

Most dynamic psychotherapies are based on the belief that the lack of closure, i.e., the inability to complete a situation, is a primary cause for much of the suffering in the world. Examples abound of people—individuals and groups—who are unable to achieve closure, who are unable to move on. Here is one:

> *Joan was married to a psychology professor who, because of his career, had to move the family to the*

south. She yearned for her childhood home in California. Her sensitive husband, though unable to move back, would have their family spend the summers there. We used to say that "Joan lives in California; she just happens to spend autumn, winter and spring in Tennessee."

Closure and Loss

Much of life is about loss. It is a constant in our lives, whether by our choice, the choice of others, or simply circumstance. We experience the loss of opportunities, of physical abilities, and of life stages. Yet for many of us, the most difficult and profound losses are relationships.

Life is a continuous process of holding on and letting go. Most of the time, the process occurs gracefully, with little awareness. However, grief often triggers a premature rupture. We are forced to end a relationship long before we are ready. As a result, we are thrown out of our rhythm. We are forced to deal with constructing a new sense of order in a revised world, and to find a new balance.

One of our basic tasks as humans is to adjust creatively to what life hands us. Every important experience contains the seeds of wisdom. It is our relationship to the loss that matters. If we prematurely move on without honoring the learning embedded in the loss, an important opportunity for growth and development has been denied. On the other hand, if we linger too long, and if the loss is constantly figural, unduly influencing and distorting the present and future, then possibilities for newness and creativity are also diminished. We are trapped in non-redemptive grief and longing, experienced as reparable only by the undoing of the loss, by the physical return of the loved one. We are held hostage by a kind of hope that has no evidence to support it, a kind of hope that translates into delayed disappointment and missed opportunities.

We all yearn for a sense of completion: a hug that ends with mutuality, a relationship that terminates with mutual consent, and a life that ends well. Yet the times when this happens are rare. At best, if we are very lucky, the pain and obsessive focus that accompanies large loss fades in time and becomes integrated into our own new and ever-changing self, receding largely into the background. The important relationships, in whatever form they manifest, never end. They are with us forever and become who we are and what we do (Melnick and Roos, 2007, p. 104).

Closure is a Myth/Unfinished Business

When we affirm that closure is a myth, we mean, as we say above, that important experiences remain with us forever, often leading to learning and development. They also sometimes result in a type of stuckness or loss of functioning. This *unfinished business* is sometimes *not just a* lack of completion, but *too much interest* in what should be past. It keeps us from moving on, from being open to new experiences. As mentioned previously, most schools of depth psychotherapy believe that unfinished business keeps us from being in the present, and inhibits growth and development.

This is not only true for our clients, but for us as interveners. As we engage with our clients our unfinished business is constantly being evoked.

Originally called *counter-transference*, this unfinished business of the therapist involves our projecting the past onto the present moment without awareness (Melnick, 2003). We often ask our students what they notice as signs of their unfinished business. Here are some of their responses.

80

Table 1

SIGNS OF UNFINISHED BUSINESS

- Being overly happy or fearful about seeing the client
- Caring *too much* about the client's issue
- Experiencing unusually strong physical reactions
- Quickly reacting to the system
- Having judgmental responses
- Feeling too responsible for our clients
- Laughing off the problem
- Holding our responses in for too long
- Experiencing sessions as unusually exhausting
- Being unaware of what is going on in the moment
- Only seeing one client and not the system
- Finding oneself deflecting or telling "war stories"
- Feeling that there are *no* choices in making an intervention
- Mind reading of clients
- Thinking we *really understand* these people and know what's good for them
- Experiencing a *halo effect* regarding how the person looks, talks, moves
- Being *mesmerized*
- Giving unsolicited advice

We should point out that these responses are ordinary. Being aware of these *triggers* allows us to value them as important to learning. And sometimes, when appropriate, sharing them with our clients allows us to create a way of talking to each other that is very different from most approaches.

We would like to note that unfinished business

often plays a significant role in problems that occur in organizations. We project not only our unfinished past with individuals onto others but also our experiences with hierarchy, leadership, and types of organizations (see *Figure 2* and *Appendix C*).

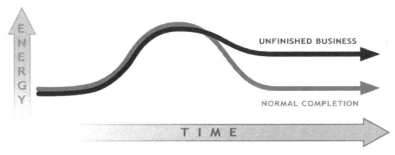

Figure 2: Unfinished Business

Loss

Although we promote the concept of closure, we can never totally complete, finish or terminate an important experience or relationship, because it continues to live in our memory. If the process flows smoothly, the previous experience largely recedes from awareness, but it is not possible to completely erase what resides within and between us. All experience, especially loss, leaves a permanent mark. How we access the memory and manage the resulting emotion is what signifies our level of growth, development, maturity, and even wisdom.

All loss is in some way relational, including self-loss (as in chronic sorrow) and loss of life stages (as in aging). A large loss casts one into a void since relationships, even very painful or conflicted ones, allow for predictability. Virtually all of us fear letting go of the familiar. It is even more difficult when the loss is traumatic and unexpected. A Gestalt approach provides support in traversing this void by helping the individual to come into contact with the experience. It can facilitate the reduction of inflexible ideals and expectations, thereby changing the potency of the life and world that should have been. It can assist the individual in realizing that the unknown future is not so unknown after all, since the past always adheres to the present and helps to shape the future. Loss is constantly the focus of diverse and changing interpretations, being reworked, usually beneficially, in terms of temporality. To paraphrase Rilke, there is value in living everything, including the questions (Melnick and Roos, 2007, p. 99).

And we conclude:

> Some say that the heart has a will of its own, far beyond the reaches of reason, and that once it is fully given it can never be fully retrieved. This premise certainly seems true when we are faced with profound loss. For many, the pain and suffering known as grief is so deep that it feels unfathomable. It is easy to see why we may wish to stop the torment at all costs—seeking templates and models that promise a re-ordering and quick relief. These are the models that offer the hope that if one works hard, acts in certain ways, and performs the necessary rituals, closure will occur. We believe that this orientation to complex endings is deeply flawed; we have attempted to show that closure, as it is commonly understood, is a myth (Melnick and Roos, p. 104).

The Evolution of the Cycle of Experience

Because experience is multidimensional, we have struggled for years to find a way to illustrate Gestalt theory in a visual form. Consequently, there have been many iterations of the original Cycle. One of the most obvious has been to transform it into a sine wave to signify that the concepts of *beginning and ending* do not exist independently, that experience is never stagnant, and that one experience moves into another. Experience, as we have said, is always ongoing, without a definitive beginning or end (*Figure 3*).

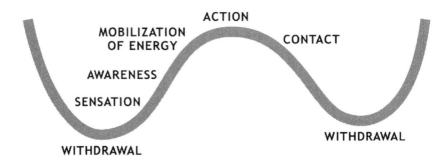

Figure 3: The Cycle of Experience as a Sine Wave
(Zinker, 1977, p. 97, reproduced with permission)

The Cycle of Experience Is
Always Reflecting Contact

Originally, contact was considered to be a specific part of the Cycle, occurring after action and followed by meaning making and withdrawal. We soon began to realize that all the stages involve contact. The difference is more in terms of the degree and direction of the energy expended. *The Cycle of Experience is, in fact, a description of a contacting process. In Figure 4* below, the vertical axis represents the movement of energy, and the horizontal axis represents time. As you can tell, contacting is happening throughout (see Nevis, 2009, p. 41).

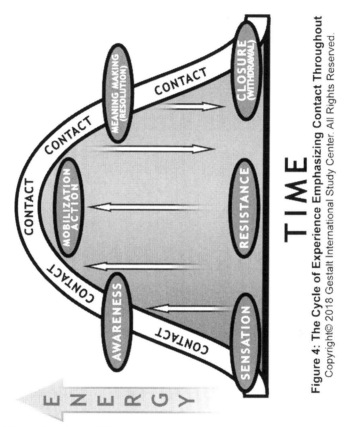

The Cycle of Experience as a Social Process

One of the biggest changes occurred when we learned to embrace a truly relational model of human experience. We understood that so-called *resistances to contact* were *just patterns* and, more importantly, always involved others. We knew that the Cycle needed to reflect the relational field. And most importantly, we

85

understood that *viewing the Cycle as an individual process is incorrect and that it had to reflect more the social and relational core of experience.*

Figure 5 represents four people engaged in a relational experience. It could be a project team at a meeting, four friends deciding where to go for dinner, or a family meeting around a family crisis. In most cases they arrive with different thoughts, feelings, energy, and recent pasts. They have to join each other, become interested in the same thing, do the work, be able to lose interest, end, and go on to the next experience.

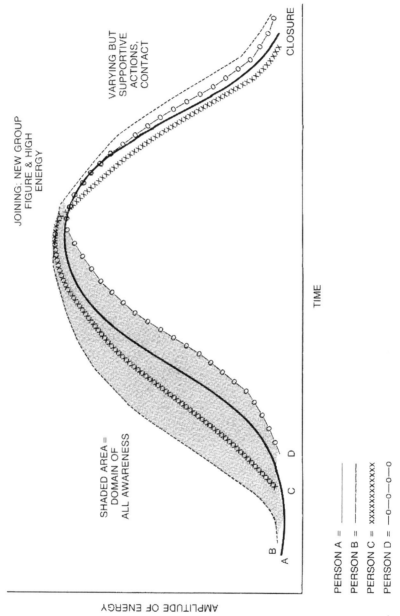

Figure 5.The Cycle of Experience with Four People
(E. Nevis, 1987, p. 53, reproduced with permission)

87

In Closing

There are many versions of the Cycle of Experience which can be used to make sense out of different situations. For example, we have used it to assist people in understanding their writing process by helping them become aware of where they move effortlessly and where they get stuck (Melnick, 2011; Fischer, 2011). One of our favorite versions of the Cycle was created by Rick Mauer (1966), who works with organizations. He has replaced *sensation* with *random incidents,* i.e., something is occurring but we aren't paying attention. *Recognition* replaces *awareness*, *initial actions* replace *mobilization* or the building up of energy, while *implementation* replaces the original contact portion of the Cycle.

The Cycle, at its core, represents a natural rhythm in which we are initially with ourselves, having an internal experience. Then we begin caring, engaging, and ending by making meaning of an experience.

6

HOW WE ORGANIZE OURSELVES

Joe: *As I look over the chapter about how our model evolved, I notice that we use the word* development *over and over again. I think that our model of development is largely about habits. It is about how we create, change, and preserve them, and how we give them up.*

Sonia: Habits *is a funny word. What do you mean? There are wonderful habits and bad habits. I don't know that we teach people about habits.*

Joe: *We make them aware of their habits: the ones they want to keep and the ones they want to get rid of or change.*

Sonia: *I think we might be talking about the same thing, but we might be using different words. We make people aware of what they are doing and what they are not doing and put them into another way of being. They learn to see things they have never seen before. They don't change. They develop and get richer.*

Joe: *But isn't development at its core about our learning how to organize and reorganize our experience?*

Sonia: *I wouldn't use the word* organize, *but I could go along with it.*

Joe: *Let me tell you what I mean. Babies have minimal abilities to organize. They quickly begin to learn what a bottle is and to recognize their mothers, but not much else at the beginning. So, development is adding more complex organizations. Does that make sense?*

Sonia: *Yes. I learned to understand this when I did a lot of work with infants. I studied them for my dissertation; how they grow and how they organize their world. Infants are so persistent. If they like something, they smile; if not they scream. They are learning, but learning is not the right word. They are saying what they need right off the bat. They cry when they cry, they sleep when they sleep. You can't make them do much of anything at this age. I think that what you call* organizing, *I call* teaching *them. Can I give you a little example? My first child was a crier all the time. As long as I held her, she wouldn't cry. What she was crying for was milk. When she was about six weeks old and would see me warming the bottle, she would stop crying.*

Joe: *Yes. That's what I am trying to say. But I am saying it differently. We both know that even with an infant who is driven primarily by biological needs, you, as her mother, are an important part of her reality right from the beginning, and she yours. And, of course, you are both organizing each other simultaneously.*

Sonia: *Still to this day, if I am feeding a child with a spoon, I have to open my mouth. I did that originally so that my daughters would open theirs. Is that what you mean by habit?*

Joe: Yes.

Development and Patterns

We are never alone. Even in the womb, the embryo is in relationship to the mother, and the mother to the embryo. And once born, the baby and caregiver are in relationship via a process of mutual influence and development. What we are saying is that development is never a solitary experience. It always takes place between the self and another. As Staemmler (2015) points out, who we are, *our self*, develops in a dialogical format. And we are not just *taking in others*. Our relational experiences become internalized and lead to the development of our sense of self.

Some of these interactions are insignificant and barely register, like a brief conversation with a cashier at the supermarket. But many are more important, demonstrating similarity and repetition, and acquiring recognizable forms that we refer to as *patterns* (Staemmler, 2015). And while having a redundancy, they are also situational, impacted by the current relational event such as the content (going to a movie, giving each other a massage, visiting our children, etc.) and the background influences.

Every situation can be viewed from a redundancy/chaos perspective. If every pattern in life were always the same across situations, there would be no growth, and if our patterns were minimally structured, at best every moment would be a new experience resulting in confusion. So, development, at its core, is the creation of patterns that are often internalized dialogues like when we are *talking to ourselves*. There is always an internalized other. Growth involves an ability to access the patterns that serve us well—given our current situation. And growth also entails adding more complex, new patterns and letting go of the ones that no longer are useful.

How We Organize

How we organize and act is greatly impacted by our needs, wants and desires, as Woody Allen points out:

It reminds me of that old joke. You know, a guy

walks into a psychiatrist's office and says, "Hey doc, my brother's crazy! He thinks he's a chicken." Then the doc says, "Why don't you turn him in?" Then the guy says, "I would, but I need the eggs." I guess that's how I feel about relationships. They're totally crazy, irrational, and absurd, but we keep going through it because we need the eggs (Allen and Brinkman, 1977).

Infants have only a primitive form of needing and organizing. For them, complex wants and desires hardly exist; they are primarily governed by their impulses. So, we talk of their world being filled with needs of a simple kind: food, sleep, nurturance, stimulation, love, soothing, contact, comfort, and support. And although even newborns demonstrate ability for preferences, they don't, to a large degree, experience separateness from their environment. Their ability to choose and organize is at a basic level. In a real sense, they *are* their needs and wants. As infants grow into children, they gradually begin to experience their separateness. It is this increasing ability to connect, differentiate, and organize that is necessary for normal childhood development (Duhigg, 2014).

Organizing can be short-term or long-term, changing from moment to moment or seemingly cast in stone. In the short-term, if I am hungry and walk into a fancy restaurant, I will most likely ignore the beautiful flowers and focus on the menu. But once I have had a little food, I will begin to pay more attention to a friend, the feel of my seat, or the people at the bar. Long-term organizing, for let's say becoming a lawyer, could impact much of one's day to day life for many years.

Relational Development

As we discussed in the last chapter, it is relatively easier to envision the process of an individual's patterned way of organizing experience—its beginning, middle, and end—than when two or more people are involved. As they attempt to be in relationship, differences begin to emerge. This is because most of us move from one experience to another at different rates. Some of us like to spend more time attending to ourselves before turning to others, while some prefer to move towards relational connections quickly. Some of us seem to know immediately which movie we wish to see, while for others it takes longer to decide. In addition, we all have different preferences and competencies, depending on the situation or context.

What we are saying is obvious. People are different in terms of how they move through the world. When we are alone, this movement can be relatively simple and easy. But we are social beings, and much of our lives are spent relationally. We have to know when and how to join and connect with another, and when to turn away and let go in such a way that works. It is much more difficult than many of us think. Behaving competently involves having *a range of movement from beginning to middle to end, depending on whom we are with and the context in which we find themselves.*

We have to bear the fact that one cost of being in a relationship is that we often don't get what we want, especially if we think of wants as simple content, such as where to eat, where to go on vacation, or whether to move forward with a project. But wants are also relational. We also want to please others and we want them to please us. We want them to give in to us and also to convince us to have another way of looking at things. We want them to respect and care about us, and we want to care about and respect them too.

Let us give a simple example of two people going out to eat in a restaurant. One wants Chinese food, while the other prefers Italian. How do they decide where to go? The negotiation of differences is just beginning here. They will have to figure out the time, the place, whether to make reservations or not, and how to get there. Once they are at the restaurant, they have to contend with important differences. One likes to order quickly, the other slowly. One likes to talk while eating; the other likes to eat in silence. One likes to share food, while the other does not. One likes to linger and have a cup of coffee, while the other likes to leave quickly.

Life is filled with everyday situations like these. Many people find a way to work it out, and many do not. But when people are experiencing relational problems, it is a good guess that they are out of sync as to how to join together to manage differences. Later, when we talk about how we work with peers, couples, teams, and organizations, you will see exactly what we teach in order to get them to a satisfying, joined experience.

A fundamental aspect of Gestalt thinking is the organism-environment relationship. It is about how human beings find out what they need to live effectively in the world they inhabit, and how to go about getting what they need. One could think of this concern as basic animal biology of the human brain and nervous system. Gestalt psychologists started out by simply studying how people perceive, but discovered very quickly that it is not a passive process. It is an active, creative activity in which needs influence what is seen or experienced (E. Nevis, 2009).

Organizing and Patterns

As stated above, the early Gestalt psychologists were concerned with perception. They were researchers who

94

were striving to make sense of how we organize experience. They understood that without an ability to organize, we would never be able to make sense of the world. They discovered a set of *perceptual laws* that, in general, apply to us all (Parlett, 1992). Yet, we still each organize differently. Some of us have a broad repertoire for organizing experience, others a narrower one; some organize only quickly, and some only slowly. Some have a need for tight organizations; others are more comfortable with loose ones. (For a description of some of these organizing principles, see Parlett, 1992.) When how we organize is less responsive to our current situation, and is redundant, we describe ourselves as having *fixed* gestalts.

Every way of organizing has its benefits and costs. For example, one problem with people who tend to organize quickly is that they might not spend enough time allowing patterns to emerge. We might label them impulsive. One challenge for people who organize slowly is that if there is a crisis, they may miss opportunities to act. We sometimes label them obsessive. One unusual way of organizing involves having associations that are not common or ordinary, resulting in meanings, understandings, and behaviors that differ dramatically from the norm. We sometimes label those who organize in this way schizophrenic, yet this way of organizing is also often true for highly creative, spiritual, and visionary individuals.

Most of our ways of organizing are not so extreme as to be labeled as schizophrenic or genius, but we all organize in our own way, and we all have to live with our differences. To develop, it is important for us to have an understanding of how we and others organize, and what our tendencies are. People in good relationships have to be able to accommodate others who organize their experience in different ways. They have to be curious about another's way of organizing

95

without being righteous or condemning. Competent people realize that habits are organizations, not truths. Here is a vignette:

Robert and John are married and work as writers. The way they organize experience is very different. Robert likes loose organizations, reads three books at a time and doesn't believe in consulting recipes or maps. John is unable to stop reading if he is in the middle of a chapter, follows directions to a T, and always shuts drawers and closes closets. John's writings follow a detailed outline, with an article never taking more than three drafts.

Robert writes two articles at a time, jumping back and forth between them. His writing process most resembles sculpting, as the shape constantly changes and evolves. He is never quite sure what it will be until it is done. His articles take many drafts.

When they were first married, they would argue over what was the right, correct, more efficient, creative, and enlightened way to write. These discussions quickly went beyond writing and would stretch across a wide range of content; the issue was never resolved.

Over time they noticed their conversation changing. They would find themselves beginning to laugh in the middle of one of these passionate discussions, as the redundancy of the disagreement caught their attention. This pause would give them the space to move away from it. Now, many years later, they have finally lost interest in this difference, somehow having given up their righteousness about the correctness of how they perform their professional tasks.

In Closing

We end this chapter with a popular example of organizing differently found in many introductory psychology books. Some people see the image as a young woman, and others as an old one. Here, the same data is organized in two different ways. Both images are there. Why do some people see one and some another? It is because we are different, at least in the moment. Then as we broaden our perception, we begin to see both images and are able to easily switch back and forth between them (see *Figure 6*).

Figure 6: Old Woman / Young Woman

7

CREATING HABITS

We live our lives creating patterns that, when repeated, transform into habits, good and bad. Sometimes the habits are in our full awareness—whether we are choosing to activate them or not—and at other times, they slip into a state of automatic pilot. For example, in a snowstorm, we might be fully present when driving our car, paying acute attention to what is occurring in our environment. However, on a clear day, we may notice that we have been moving forward for several minutes completely unaware that we were behind the wheel of a car.

What Are Habits?

Habits are recurrent patterns and behaviors that have become background and largely out of our awareness. This allows us to continue living in the moment without too much reflection and analysis. Habits free us up to continue on to the next experience. This is not to cast aspersions on the process of self-reflection, but this activity must not occur too frequently, or we would be trapped in our heads, spending more time on contemplation, instead of on just being. We don't wish to become like the centipede, who when asked, "Which leg goes first?" was never able to walk again. We rely on habits for a free flowing, at times uninterrupted, existence. To reiterate, personal growth and development are dependent on the creation of habits that serve us well. But equally important is an ability to change or let go of habits when they are no longer useful or relevant to our current lives.

Sonia: *Let me tell you a little story. When Edwin was in school at Columbia he had me take some projective tests. What was shocking was that all I saw were flowers. So even then I never wanted to deal with those negative things, and I still don't. I have experienced many bad things in my life, and I have learned to let them all go.*

Joe: *So, you developed a habit of letting go of or ignoring bad things. Would you tell me how you did that?*

Sonia: *I'm not quite sure. I was told that when I was four years old I ran into the park. I met someone who had a lemon, and I traded my shoes for the lemon. I never got the shoes back, and I didn't care. I ran right over what I didn't like and moved to what I did like.*

Joe: *I'm confused. Are you saying you didn't like your shoes, or that you were attracted to a lemon and found a way to get it?*

Sonia: *Yes, I was attracted to the lemon. The way I think about it is that I learned to go to things I like, and I don't move towards things I don't like. They never did find my shoes.*

Joe: *I think you're making my point. As an aside, I've always admired your attraction to people some might label as "lemons." You have an ability to find the sweetness in them. But this is an example of a habit you like and don't have a wish to change.*

Sonia: *That is correct.*

We also need to learn to replace the habits that cause us pain, and if we can't, to live with the ones that are just too hard to change. But even for the habits we like and want to keep, we can't take them for granted.

Without awareness and practice, it is easy for them to become background and seemingly disappear.

Usefulness of Habits

All habits start out as being useful. This is even true for those that we eventually pay a big price for having—like chronically lying or drinking too much. It is easy to forget that our ability to lie creatively helped get us out of some tight situations, and that drinking proved to be very useful in helping us get over our shyness in social situations. By the time we realize the cost, however, we have often forgotten that this habit was originally an adaptive response to a situation—and the best we could do in the moment.

As a result, a habit which was once our friend can, at worst, turn into our enemy and, at best, become non-productive. Rather than destroy or extinguish it, we have to do the opposite. We have to reestablish our relationship with it. *It is the relationship which has to be different, because the basic problem in trying to change a habit is that you can't destroy it.* The habit is still there and will always be there, if not in our immediate awareness, then certainly in our memory and body.

We are always all that we have ever been. We cannot erase ourselves. What we can all learn to do is to develop other habits that break up the old patterns, by making them different, more complex, and varied. This gives us more options and, of course, we have to learn to bear the yearning for the old habit.

Joe: *But I see you as having many soft habits and not being that attached to very many things. Can you tell me one habit you tried to change and struggled with?*

Sonia: *Well, one that is clear, I never thought of as a habit. For many reasons, I grew up never*

101

speaking to anyone, and no one spoke to me. Growing up, it was not so unusual for children to be quiet. It took me a long time to change that pattern.

Joe: *To try to fit your example into what I am talking about, you developed a habit of remaining quiet and not speaking. That habit still exists in you. I know that you can stay quiet for long blocks of time. And you seem to do it easily.*

Sonia: *That's true. Interesting.*

Joe: *But for you to develop in a different way, you also had to add the ability to speak—but ability isn't what I mean.*

Sonia: *I was willing . . .*

Joe: *What do you mean willing?*

Sonia: *I don't know.*

Joe: *I'm thinking about new habits. For example, the person who wishes to lose weight has to be willing to give up late-night snacks. If they are not willing, then the game is over before it has begun. As another example, we know that sometimes people call our offices, and just the phone call and expression of willingness to look at their situation often will shift things. Whether this is permanent or not, who knows?*

Sonia: *Yes, but if it is just about willing, it won't work. There has to be more for most of us.*

Joe: *More what?*

Sonia: *That's a great question. I believe that there have to be actions, often in the form of other habits that can compete with the first one. And lots of support for when the original habit creeps back into our body.*

How Do Habits Develop?

Habits develop at a very young age because children only know what they have been taught. If we learn that we have to drink milk or we won't become strong, or if we don't brush our teeth, we'll develop cavities, then we end up doing these things without thinking. We may even end up forgetting why we developed them, and why they are still useful.

Certain habits are good for us and we want to keep them. It is good to brush our teeth, take a shower once a day, eat vegetables, kiss our mother good night, and not bite anybody. Other habits outgrow their usefulness. We need to learn to give up the pacifier, and when to cry and when to hold back tears. Throughout life it is important to decide which habits to keep and which to examine to see if they are still relevant to our current lives.

Most early habits are taught to us by adults. Much of growing up involves becoming increasingly aware of what we are doing—of our habits—and seeing if they are still useful. For example, many of us have had parents and teachers who have taught us to respect our elders, which is a good way to be most of the time. But what happens when an elder is abusive to you? What do you do? The habit of unconditional respect for elders doesn't fit here. We have to stop and explore the whole situation, to see it as more nuanced and complex. What will happen if we challenge them, report them, tell someone else, or say nothing? What are the consequences of responding in the old or new ways? What is it like to give up the easy habit of *respecting our elders*?

Groups and organizations also develop habits. Suppose you are in a meeting and see people blaming each other and apparently not listening? You notice that they continue to talk even though they are not getting a response. This seems normal and ordinary to them; the way life is. In fact, we might label this habit of blaming (projecting the negative onto others) and minimal responsiveness as part of their organizational culture— a series of unaware habits, lived without much thought or attention.

In the beginning, the development of habits helps bring the couple, family, work group, or organization together and provides the cultural glue. *All habits, at least initially, are attempts to manage a situation and have a positive side.* In the above example, you might appreciate the ability of the organizational members to express themselves freely and say hard things to each other. Families need to figure out when to clean the kitchen and how to hang the towels. Organizations have to decide what appropriate dress is, whether to keep their office doors open or closed, and what is acceptable language.

Growth and Development of Habits

Personal growth and development derive from the acquisition of new, often more complicated and nuanced, habits, and letting go of old ones that are no longer working. If we don't change and grow, we become stagnant and die—if not physically, then psychologically. This is not just true for individuals, but for couples, families, groups, and organizations. Unfortunately, in many circumstances, there is resistance to changing habits and a type of *dead man walking* phenomenon occurs—sometimes found in long-term marriages. In these situations, people have stopped noticing, seeing, smelling, listening, and touching. In these cardboard-like relationships that are filled with predictability and staleness, little new happens. Auto-pilot default is the order of the day.

One problem that occasionally arises is the

tendency to overuse what we do well, even when it is not working. So, the long-range shooting basketball player will look for similar spots to shoot from when she is covered, rather than passing the ball or driving to the basket. An organization that is strong on creating strategic plans will create them over and over again, if the current plan is not working, rather than look to create greater connection and teamwork among the associates.

> **Joe:** *A client of mine directed a high school orchestra. He once told me why the musical performance often deteriorates as the evening wears on. "It's not because the students get tired or lose their concentration. As crazy as it seems, we start at the same beginning piece of music at each practice session and rarely devote as much time to learning the later ones. By the time we get to those, practice is usually over. And as much as I am aware of this, and as much power as I have over the students, I forget to change it."*

The Persistent Nature of Habits

It is well known that problematic mannerisms, long under control and even forgotten, have an annoying propensity for re-emerging. These include: fidgeting, nail-biting, twisting the hair, counting certain items in a room, chewing on the sides of the tongue, tapping, rocking, and so on. After months of concentration on removal of a mannerism and even replacing it with an antagonistic, alternative behavior, one is not guaranteed that the fix is permanent. Insidiously, the mannerism may reappear. Skinner believed that this recurrence of long-extinguished habits is a general characteristic of learning, which he called spontaneous recovery (Melnick and Roos, 2007, p. 94).

Joe: *So, what I'm saying is that* habits live in the body. *The habit you developed of opening your mouth when feeding a child still sits inside of you—even if you are usually not aware of it. And an important part of our theory, I believe, is that we never lose a habit. It is part of who we are, even if we haven't been aware of it for years.*

Sonia: *Joe, that's very interesting. I can't quite make sense of what you are saying. We never give habits up? Did you mean that?*

Joe: *Yes. Let me give you another example. A good friend stopped smoking 45 years ago. Every once in a while, she feels an urge to smoke a cigarette, although I believe the chances of her smoking are close to zero. I believe that one reason why it is so hard to get rid of so many of our bad habits, and why relapse is so prevalent, is because for most people, the seed of the habit is still alive inside of us. This is why they say in Alcoholics Anonymous (AA) that there is no such thing as an ex-alcoholic.*

Sonia: *So, are you saying we can't do anything about changing habits we want to change?*

Joe: *No. I am saying that the notion that we can permanently extinguish habits is largely a fool's errand. Habits (and desires which provide the fuel for most habits) live in our bodies and in our minds; most of the time with very little awareness.*

Sonia: *That's an interesting thought.*

Joe: *It's funny that you should say so. I thought it was originally yours. If we take what I am saying as a possibility, then I hope people would be relieved rather than depressed.*

Sonia: *Oh, it never occurred to me to be depressed. I thought it was pretty interesting; that a habit could be there and usable.*

Joe: *Yes. But I wasn't talking about the good habits, like arriving on time or remembering to tell your children that you love them. I meant the negative habits, like always finding a way to avoid exercising.*

To repeat, even though habits may fade into the background, they are never extinguished. They still have the potential to emerge, not only under stressful conditions, but also ones of joy and pleasure. Knowing that old habits don't go away permanently allows us to not be surprised or discouraged when they reappear. Knowing that this is possible lets us return more easily to our newer habits.

Our habits may be so ingrained that they can seem to present an almost impenetrable barrier to change. For example, our most experienced students often have greater trouble learning our model. This consistently surprised us until we began to understand that their experience and competence were getting in the way of the new learning. Their abilities, whether being well versed at understanding the inner life of an individual or at problem solving, made it more difficult to focus on the *in between* of people. Also, they found it hard to shift *from* paying attention to and working with the problems that people present, *to watching for people's competencies,* i.e., *for what they do well.* Their habit of focusing on what's wrong was getting in the way of new learning. It is often easier to learn something new and different when you don't have to *unlearn*.

Habits and Addictions

Addictions too fall under this category of persistent habits. *Much of what we call addictions are simply unrelenting wants and needs that have been organized into patterns highly resistant to feedback and change. If they start out as positive, while undermining our sense of well-being, they are compulsively done anyway in the end.* Until recently, we differentiated between *physical addiction* to substances like alcohol and cocaine, and *behavioral "addictions"* like gambling and shopping which were strong, difficult-to-change habits. However, the latest neurological research indicates that, if you put someone in front of a slot machine, their brain will look qualitatively the same as someone shooting heroin (Alter, 2017).

People "addicted" to exercise will not pay attention to whether they are tired or their foot aches, or notice the person on the stationary bicycle beside them. These insatiable *wants* are so ingrained and deeply *grooved* that they narrow our lives, making us oblivious to other things that are co-occurring. Here is another vignette:

> *Mary had struggled with weight her entire life. She ping-ponged back and forth between being thin and heavy. She told me of a recent meeting she had gone to that had shaken her up. As the meeting started, someone brought in a box of doughnuts and placed them on a side table. From then on, the meeting was a blur. All she could think about were the doughnuts. She swears that they even started talking to her saying, "Eat me. Eat me."*

Joe: *I believe that if we don't create opposing habits—let's say of making sure that there is no liquor around, of calling a sponsor,* *praying, playing an inspirational recording, or exercising—which can compete with the re-energized original habit of drinking too much, we are at greater risk of falling back or, as we say, "falling off the wagon."*

Sonia: *I hate that phrase "falling off the wagon," and I know why. The idea of falling off the wagon implies some painful, hurtful experience; a loss of awareness, control, willpower. We are constantly falling off wagons; it is part of being human. What we learn as we fall off and get up is what is important. In terms of what you said, it just happened to me now. I didn't want to take another piece of chocolate, but I just took it. I didn't blame myself. I am nice to myself.*

Joe: *Yes, I know that about you. To use the same language, you were limiting yourself to one piece, and when you took a second, you fell off the wagon.*

Sonia: *I never would have thought about that phrase in a million years. I said "OK."*

Joe: *I notice that you also shrugged your shoulders.*

Sonia: *The words that go with my shrug are, "That's the way it goes."*

Joe: *Yes. It's crazy to punish ourselves when we fall off the wagon—as if making ourselves feel bad works. Yet feeling bad about myself when I mess up is so ingrained in me and in most people I know. As I say this, I realize that I have developed other habits to soothe myself when I fall off the wagon which, like everyone else, I do numerous times a day.*

Sonia: *So, what do you do that makes it easier for you to feel okay when you do something that you don't like?*

Joe: *I laugh at myself for being so unforgiving. I tease myself, saying that I am so important that I have to devote so much energy into feeling bad. Like many, I learned at a young age the habit of feeling bad and being unforgiving of myself and of others.*

Sonia: *Can I tell you what I did? I haven't thought of it for a while. Whenever I mess up, I always say the same thing. I say, "I don't deserve to be hung by my thumbs."*

Joe: *That's great. So how did you learn to be that way?*

Sonia: *I don't know. I know that I never want to be mean to myself. I've had enough meanness in my life.*

Joe: *What's interesting is that you don't seem to know how you learned it, but you do have a skill of saying a sentence or two to yourself that works.*

Sonia: *And that is true. I feel the same thing for others. I don't go to feeling bad when there is nothing I can do about it.*

In Closing

As interveners, we approach our work with an open stance from which we bracket off our past values, beliefs, assumptions, and experience as best we can. We do this so that we can focus on the system's process in the form of relational patterns. Much of development involves creating patterns that turn into habits, thus allowing us to focus on the next moment. These habits are often out of our awareness, feeling almost reflexive and as much of who we are as our skin and bones. Nearly all habits start out as positive, but often become *overdeveloped* and are used when other responses and behaviors would be better suited for the situation.

Once we become aware of our habits, change can follow, for we have a choice: accept them as they are; or attempt to alter them, often by adding new habits. Of course this is difficult, as we have said repeatedly, since old habits never die. In the next chapter, we will discuss how to change habits, and how to acquire important skills to implement those changes.

8

MANAGING AND CHANGING HABITS

Learning to Change Habits

Paradoxical Theory of Change

A good way to change a habit is to enter fully into the experience. If you smoke, slowly smell and taste the smoke, feel the cigarette touching your fingertips, and experience the craving fully, you will notice a flickering of change. This approach was revolutionary when first introduced, and was in contrast to others that viewed bad habits as failures of willpower. *The paradoxical theory of change states that awareness leads to change* (Beisser, 1970). We believe that this awareness opens up choices, and it is the experience of choice that is essential for growth and development. Beisser's theory has received wide support, and is fundamental to many of the contemporary approaches to dealing with trauma and addiction.

> **Joe**: *I once worked with a start-up organization that had a cultural habit of always valuing expansion. At a retreat which was set up to decide whether to build a new office building, they became aware of how the old habit of having fun, which initially had brought them together, might be lost if they had to drastically increase revenue to pay for new offices. They quickly decided to stay in the old building complex and use a portion of their available funds to refurbish their current facility. They then spent the rest of the retreat playing golf and reconnecting. Their increased awareness of the costs and benefits of*

building a new space allowed them to clarify their values and make a choice.

Awareness stirs up energy that is close to the surface. Rather than teaching our clients to get rid of the sensation, we teach them to heighten what they are actually doing. We teach them a way to experience their sensations, not just their thoughts. *When you are aware, possibilities emerge, and your energy is free to land in a different place.* As long as *you* are unaware of *your* habits, *you* can't choose. By helping our clients to see possibilities, we are giving them choices. Many therapists and change agents would be urging them instead to stop what they are doing. We believe differently. *Only when you begin to experience a habit fully do you recognize the possibility of a choice and have a chance to chan*ge. For example, people with an extremely obsessive style are people who are so wedded to their habits that their everyday lives are hampered. There is a popular television show that focuses on the lives of hoarders—people who compulsively acquire or refuse to dispose of objects until the habit leaves no room for anything or anyone else, both physically and relationally. Many excessively obsessive people are in mental hospitals, counting to a thousand over and over again, or washing their hands 500 times a day. Rather than try to stop the hand washing, a colleague of ours helped them notice that each time they washed their hands, they were doing it differently (Todd Burley, personal communication, 2010). Sometimes they splashed their hands in the water, sometimes they lathered soap a lot, sometimes a little, sometimes they shifted their legs, sometimes their bodies were still. Noticing that their repetitive actions were already changing, if ever so slightly, helped them begin to shift. Becoming aware that they were not totally controlled by the obsession provided the opportunity to do things differently. Once they noticed, they had the potential to change.

Habits Are Hard to Change

Learning to ride a bicycle or drive a car are skills that take time to acquire; once learned, they become part of our routine. We do them well without thinking. But we can all remember back to our feelings the first time we got behind the wheel of a car, when the skill of driving had not yet become automatic.

It is a challenge to change habits. Our society teaches us an approach that can best be described as a two-step dance. We learn to move either towards the positive or away from the negative; either to increase or diminish. It is easy to forget that habits are essential parts of who we are. *What we are not taught in our culture is to become interested in our habits as processes which have a dynamic life and the potential to change and evolve—the potential to teach us something.* Learning to become interested is what generates awareness and the possibility for change.

The *deep rootedness* of many habits accounts for how difficult they are to alter; whether it is within ourselves or with others. Instead of focusing on changing a habit, we begin by examining its original usefulness. It is easy to forget that every habit, no matter how "good" or "bad," has a nugget of competence in it. Once we understand that all habits begin as our best attempt to derive pleasure or solve a problem, we can look at the price we now pay. Understanding that there is a steep cost still does not make it easy to change a habit, but it helps.

Common examples are New Year's resolutions. Many of us promise to drink less, exercise more, eat healthier, call our parents once a week, etc. We wish to be different because we believe that, if we could change these things, our lives would be better. In the exuberance and tradition of New Year's, we forget the value of the old habits and the cost of change—to give up those wonderful times of lying in bed in order to exercise, or to deprive ourselves of the joy of the hot fudge sundae, or the delicious taste of that glass of wine. Research indicates that giving ourselves a break and accepting our imperfections is important, given that nearly nine out of ten resolutions fail (Wiseman, 2007).

Substituting and Changing Focus

Rather than focusing on changing a habit, it is often easier to substitute another one. Many replace smoking with chewing gum, going to an AA meeting instead of going to a bar, or eating fruit instead of ice cream. If a child is being hit repeatedly by a peer, we can teach the child to fight back and ask for help. And we can teach the hitter to hit a pillow instead of someone else. Everyone wins: the child being hit, the hitter, and the parents.

This notion of focusing on something else and not heightening the sensation or feeling is also basic to dealing with chronic pain or trauma. Our original approach of *reliving the trauma with support* often does not work (Taylor, 2013). To learn when to turn away and when to enter experience is a core skill of competent adults. wherefore the above suddenly??

A common example of this dynamic for most therapists deals with people who experience bouts of low self-esteem. Let's say that these clients have had enough psychotherapy to understand the historical reasons for where, when, and why they developed such negative feelings. They understand that they are extremely sensitive to feeling bad about themselves. It is a self-defeating habit. All this knowledge, though useful, is sometimes not enough. During these times of feeling bad, their sense of competence is diminished for a variety of reasons, some rational, some not. As a result, they go into a downward spiral, blaming themselves and others. They know that they need to do something different in these moments, but they don't know what. They have to develop an effective response to the internalized negative voice that tells them that they are not good enough.

For most of us, poor self-esteem occurs when we cannot generate enough internal and external support to feel good about who we are. We have a heightened sense of feeling bad. Frozen, we are unable to move towards possibilities. Instead of being caught up in feeling bad, we need to figure out an action; something to do that will help us feel a little bit better. For example, we could carry a [$100] bill in our pocket and whenever we are feeling *poorly*, take it out, look at it, and touch it. Another possibility is for us to get a wallet full of [dollar] bills, walk around, and give them out to people who could use them. If successful, these experiences allow people to shift their habits and to become more comfortable by receiving different supports, both from themselves and others. And, of course, if our clients are resistant to trying new behaviors, that process becomes the therapeutic work.

Because it is very difficult to undo a habit, especially one that has had a long life, it is much easier to learn a new one. When we learn new things we usually feel good, and the old patterns begin to loosen their hold on us, physiologically, intellectually, psychologically, and emotionally. *Knowing how to develop new and different ways of being in the world is an important competency skill.* And as we learn and get support for new habits, we often lose interest in the old ones. If we are lucky, they fade into the background. But that doesn't mean that the habit is gone forever.

Changing the Background

Rather than changing the habit we can change the background, the *surround*. For example, Alcoholics Anonymous teaches people to not have alcohol in the house and not to go to places where liquor is served. We also know that, if we associate with people who have *bad* habits, we are likely to acquire them, as we also would with people who have *good* ones. Take, for instance, a colleague who is an exercise nut: he gets up at 5:00 every day, rain or shine, to work out a minimum of one and a half hours at the gym. Interestingly, when he is traveling, which he often is, he can't seem to get up in the morning and exercise, even though he chooses hotels that have fitness centers. So, a different environment supports a change, albeit temporary, in his exercise habit.

Skills for Managing and Changing Habits

As we have suggested earlier, being aware and understanding how and why a habit originally developed, although important for change, is often not enough. If it were, life would be a lot easier for all of us. Change usually requires more; a set of skills that goes beyond understanding. Here are three important skills: *commitment, effort, and discipline.*

- *Commitment*
Commitment does not exist independently in a vacuum. If we are living a good, rich life, we will have many competing wants. It is easy to overly commit ourselves, especially to those wants that require little initial effort and result in quick gratification, without realizing the effort it may eventually take. As a result, focus may be siphoned away from the wants that ultimately matter

most.

Often, we not only make commitments too easily, but we also tend to make them too quickly. This is because the actual act of making the commitment, in and of itself, is satisfying and brings relief.[17] "I promise not to lie anymore, to stop drinking, and to be nicer to you." It simply feels good to speak a commitment or to write it down. It is hard to beat this simple and quick, but fleeting, form of satisfaction.

It is also difficult to keep commitments because we live in a society that views the flow of life primarily by one standard: success or failure. We overvalue success and so are not taught how to live well with our failures, despite the fact that for every success there are often multiple losses. We all fail every day, thus experiencing disappointment and bad feelings. Our challenge is to accept disappointments as commonplace and to learn to be friendly with the parts of ourselves and others that do not meet our idealistic standards.

Lastly, we reiterate that commitments are not made in a vacuum. Our relationship with ourselves, friends, lovers, and colleagues is constantly changing. We are continuously confronted with the temporariness of our situation. To keep an ongoing commitment, we need to be able to stay on course, knowing that we will be persistently challenged by life's changing landscape (Melnick and S. Nevis, 2006).

Making a commitment to change an old habit or initiate a new behavior implies a promise. In order to meet these commitments, we must first pay more attention to the making and breaking of them, for

---

[17] Much research suggests that announcing goals diminishes the chances of achieving them. It supplies satisfaction and decreases motivation (Wicklund and Gollwitzer, 1981).

commitments too easily made are also too easily broken. For most, it is easy to make a promise, because of our wish to feel good about ourselves, to please others, to decrease tension, or to avoid conflict. However, we tend to underestimate the cost involved in keeping it. When we break a commitment, it behooves us to do it well, so as not to damage the relationship—with ourselves and others—more than necessary. A broken promise, when acknowledged and owned fully, provides opportunities for personal growth and relational development, as elucidated in the following citation:

> If the relational nature of promises gets forgotten or is avoided, or if it is not addressed by all involved, a trail of poor connections can result. It is not enough for one individual to acknowledge the breaking of a promise: "I know I said that I would write weekly, and I often intend to, but the truth is that I am not doing it." The other must also have a responsibility to the promise and the relationship. "I notice that your writing is becoming sparse and the content feels perfunctory. I want us to deal with it." (Melnick and S. Nevis, 2006b, p. 32).

Ultimately though, learning to make thoughtful promises and to own the impact of the broken ones, while important, is not enough. There has to be ongoing effort and discipline to carry us through the times when easy energy simply isn't there.

- *Effort*

The *making of the promise*, the saying of "I am going to do it," generates a quick sense of joy and optimism that is short lived when the quick exuberance fades. It is at this point that we often begin to doubt our good sense in making the promise at all, as we become aware of the cost of keeping it. Often, we realize that we made the promise too quickly and misjudged the necessary effort, or in hindsight we realize that we have other things that we would like to do more. Sometimes we simply *forget.*

At this point, we need to acknowledge that we might wish we hadn't made the promise in the first place. In order to keep the promise, we must draw on our skills to stay the course, to experiment, to learn new behaviors, and to hold on to the initial promise as valuable and worthwhile. At these moments, when our good intentions come face to face with the effort necessary for growth and maintenance, much learning occurs. During these times, we shape much of our lives.

- *Discipline*

Commitment involves being able to stay on course. This is not only true of loving and working, but exercising, meditating, and saying difficult things. To support ourselves in the face of distractions or competing attractions, to resist the pull of other events and to overcome inertia and boredom requires discipline.

Discipline involves practice. We need to do the behavior many times so that it becomes embedded in us. A good example is learning to drive. In time, we become less aware of braking, turning, etc. Driving becomes automatic. However, we all occasionally veer off course. At these moments, discipline involves an ability to acknowledge the breakdown and return to performing the actions until they reinforce the habit again.

When Nothing Works

Sometimes awareness, good intentions, and practice still do not work. *Trying to stop* often fails because the habit is so strong. "Yes, I may die of cancer, but I still can't stop smoking." At that point, for many of us, the work of trying to stop is over. *Competency involves knowing how to accept the power of the habit, rather than making ourselves miserable by trying and failing over and over again to do something different.*[18] There is something intrinsically potent about accepting *what is,* even if it is the powerlessness to change. Acceptance is, in fact, a change in the individual, even if the powerful habit remains. *Our tasks as adults is to learn to live with habits that do not serve us well.*

As mentioned above, *not only is awareness sometimes not enough; we now understand that it can sometimes cause harm.* This is because deeply grooved habits have tremendous energy in them and, as we have said repeatedly, remain within us, often forever (Duhigg, 2014). Becoming aware of yearning for the sensations and behaviors might actually lead to doing them, or at least cause some pain and suffering. Often, gamblers still dream and yearn for the *big win* many years after they have supposedly *kicked* the habit. Funny how many of us yearn for our old love, even though that person may have treated us poorly. *The ability to not caricature desires and to experience and live well with our yearnings is a high-level skill.*

We are all products of a society which values certain ways of defining, judging, and labeling deep-seated yearnings. In our modern Western culture, a high value is placed on objects of desire—not on desiring as an ongoing process. We make the mistake

---

[18] Research indicates that people who know how to be supportive of others often are judgmental about their own failures and inadequacies (Neff, 2011). In addition, learning to give ourselves a break results in less anxiety and depression and leads to more optimism and happiness (Parker-Pope, 2011).

of putting the emphasis on the figure, while largely ignoring the ground.

We learn to project our desires onto the world and then go after them. If we don't achieve satisfaction and success, we are to try harder. We are taught that satisfaction comes from winning, i.e., getting our desires met.

Not only are we taught to treat our desires as things, but also to label them. We learn to use negative words such as addiction or obsession for cravings which cause obvious pain to ourselves and others. We appropriately view these behaviors negatively. However, these labels sometimes become generalized to the individual. This often results in the person being seen in a narrow and rigid way and thus identified as alcoholic, workaholic, co-dependent, or sex-addicted. The person becomes a simplified caricature, devoid of other behaviors and characteristics (J. Melnick, S. Nevis, and G. Melnick, 1995).

In Closing

We need to acquire skills in order to change habits. In this chapter, we highlighted three: making and breaking commitments, effort, and discipline. Behaving competently involves knowing how to notice habits and determining which work and which do not. It requires the ability to choose which to keep, which to change, which to expand, and which to eliminate. In truth, *making a habit of noticing our habits leads to a better life.* In addition, living well in the world also means making accommodations for others who organize their experience differently and demonstrate different habits. We have to be curious about another's way of organizing without being righteous or condemning. *Competent people realize that habits are organizations and not truths.* We also need to recognize the value of seeking help from others in managing our habits, since going it alone is rarely successful.

Sonia: *The real advantage of good connections is that everyone will give you feedback about how they feel about your habits. People will tell you. They will say, "Stop doing that," or "It makes me crazy," or "I have thought about how that makes me feel."*

Joe: *I agree. It's very hard to change a habit alone. That's why so many of the successful habit-changing approaches place tremendous importance on others in the form of sponsors, coaches, trainers, therapists, ministers, groups, churches, and communities. We are substituting other habits—often relational ones—that compete with the deep-seated ones in our minds and bodies.*

Here are some final thoughts and reflections on habits.
- Habits are always relational, if not with others, then with ourselves.
- Rather than simply trying to stop a habit, we have to be able to consider other options.
- Most habits start out as our friends, but sometimes become our enemies. Then the downside of the habit becomes dominant. *A competent person notices when a once useful habit begins making trouble.*
- We have to stop blaming ourselves for having the habit and not being able to stop it. Blaming rarely helps.
- Practice is essential for changing habits, because they live in our bodies.
- We need to trust and support each other, because maintaining good habits and letting go of destructive ones is difficult to do in isolation.

- Above all, new experiences will lead us to a rich life. It is a rich life that helps soften habits, and allows for new possibilities.

So how do we, in our Cape Cod Training Program, approach habits? As practitioners of our Cape Cod model, we view our job as first seeing habits that may have been originally useful to our clients, then helping them to see those habits too, and finally supporting them in figuring out whether the habits are still good or are making trouble. This exploration often sets the stage for new behaviors (patterns and habits) to emerge and is essential for people to develop.

SECTION TWO

EXPANDING THE CAPE COD MODEL
TO LARGER SYSTEMS

INTRODUCTION

The Expansion of the Cape Cod Model

As we started to work more and more with teams and organizations, we began to realize that the goals of an organization go beyond connection and relationship. In fact, there has to be a product, a job completed that rests on a strategic planning process. There has to be goal setting.

Consequently, we recognized a need to enhance the components of our model and theory in order to better address the dynamics of hierarchical and complex systems. The chapters in this section detail our model's evolution from a couple-centric approach to one applicable to families, teams, various groups, and organizations. We devote Chapter 9 to the concepts of Strategy/Intimacy and Chapter 10 to Power, Hierarchy, and Leadership.

As our model expanded into the organizational domain, we found ourselves spending a lot of time trying to understand how the following lenses—strategy/intimacy and hierarchy/power—might shed some light on how people engage and relate to each other. We first started to study intimacy because many of the people who were taking our programs—including couples, peers, friends or co-workers—were having difficulties. We knew we had to find a way for them to learn how to talk, listen, and become interested in each other. At first, these may not seem to be skills to be learned, because we often assume that everyone has them. But this is not true. Fortunately, they can be learned, and we spent many years discovering what these skills were and how to teach them.

9

STRATEGY / INTIMACY

We originally designed our program to train therapists to help couples and families live better lives. By so doing, we began to see that the ability to form good connections (intimacy), though essential, was not enough for good relationships to develop. Of all the differences that emerge when a couple becomes a family, one of the most important is the family becoming more of a work unit with tasks to be done and people to be managed. Families have to develop plans, skills, and strategies to get the work done; goals need to be set and met. Many daily decisions involving everyone have to be made, attended to, and managed. Food has to be cooked, and money has to be earned and spent. House repairs have to be made, cars have to be maintained, and taxes paid. People in ongoing relationships have to be able to resolve issues in ways that work for everybody.

> **Sonia:** *One day after we were married I had to go to the bathroom and Ed said, "Are you mad at me?" I was stunned. I understood that, from that point on, I had the responsibility to tell someone what I was doing. I realized then that when there was garbage in the house, we had to decide who would take it out. I began quickly to see the burden of marriage. People have a life before they become a couple. And they have images about how to be a couple based on their previous lives. For most of us, this lived reality is far different from anything we have imagined.*

The World of Work

Life is more than just about connecting and deciding. Much of what is precious in life is about *doing*; and doing requires a new set of skills. We came to understand that we needed to focus more on the *doing* parts of relationships, such as commitment, effort, and discipline—those elements that we discussed in the previous chapter.

When a couple becomes a family, roles become more fixed, and these roles—of mother and father, son and daughter—reflect a series of *responsibilities that are essential for the family to thrive.* Once there are children, the parents become in charge of their health, protection, and education. No matter what we wish, children cannot adequately protect or educate themselves, nor can they do the taxes. A parent cannot become a child, nor a child a parent.

Because we were all skilled family therapists, teaching our students how to deal with the biological and relatively fixed differences between parents and children and the *doing* of work seems relatively easy in retrospect. But something else was happening that challenged our beliefs and pushed us out of our comfort zone.

During the 1980s, we began to notice an important change at our Center. As our reputation grew, more and more non-therapists came to us to learn. They came from professions such as medicine, business, and the quickly expanding fields of human resources and organizational development. They told us that what we were teaching had relevance to their professional lives. And more importantly, they challenged us to expand our concepts beyond the intimate realm of couples and families. They were interested in the world where achieving goals and producing products was most important. They came to us because, just as with families, the world of work was also changing, becoming less hierarchical and more collaborative. These leaders were finding that the people who worked for them were becoming more and more resistant to simply following without being included in the decision-making. Here is a vignette:

Abe worked as a cutter in the garment industry of New York. His job was to walk back and forth alongside a long table, rolling out bales of fabric and cutting it into many layers. He would then place a paper template that looked like the pieces of a puzzle on top of the fabric and, following the markings, begin to slowly cut the many layers into pieces. After he finished with each puzzle piece, he would tie the pieces of cloth together and pass them along to the seamstresses who would connect the patterns and turn them into dresses.

This industry was highly structured at that time, much like an assembly line, and hierarchical with the boss at the top. The cutter was next. Then came the person in charge of the seamstresses (the foreman/forewoman), and last the seamstresses themselves. But Abe wasn't a traditional cutter. He refused to punch a time clock and insisted on keeping his own time. He also insisted on having his own key to the plant and, breaking tradition, calling everyone by their first names. When the plant closed suddenly without warning, he did not express anger at the owners. He knew that all had done the best they could, as he viewed work as a partnership. Although a lifelong union man, he refused to believe that front line and management had an inherently antagonistic relationship. The trust, collaboratively developed over the years, allowed for a respectful ending.

Leaders came to us because they understood that new ways were essential to lead and manage a work force. The old leader/follower dynamic was not working, and new skills had to be learned. Until subordinates could feel respect for the leaders and, in turn, feel that the leaders respected them, they would be reluctant to follow. Followers would first have to believe that what a leader promised them was authentic. Leaders needed to understand how essential it was to build trust through relationships in order for people to follow them. They came to us to learn how to create this trust by acquiring the skills we had for many years taught as an essential component of developing *intimacy.*

But intimacy alone was not enough. Leaders also required skills to help their organizations create business plans, provide services, and get the job done. These skills fell under the label of *strategy.* It became clear to us and to the leaders who came to us that *intimacy/strategy* were conjoined twins, connected at the hip. Both were essential for creating relational and work satisfaction (Cuddy, Kohut, and Neffinger, 2013).

> **Sonia:** *During one of our training sessions, a group that had been practicing our model sat around talking with me. They could see that the model worked and was useful, but they needed something more to hold it together. This is what I told them: "Most of the time, it is essential to become interested in your workforce because interest is essential for trust, and trust is necessary for work to get done. But trust alone is not enough; everyone needs goals." "Oh," they said, "there are two parts to this model. We thought that there was only one." They agreed that the first was around connection, the intimate part—and the second about getting the*

work done, the strategic part; I immediately said, "You are right. Both are essential for every relationship, whether peer or hierarchical."

Over time, we devoted ourselves to putting into words how to make this process run smoothly. We emphasize that leaders of families and organizations have to be well practiced at and able to teach their followers both intimate and strategic skills for their group to function optimally. When learned well, these sets of abilities generate values and norms that result in vibrant, resilient, and highly functioning families and organizations.

Intimate/Strategic Lenses as Polarities

We have found that when our clients, when in trouble—be they individuals, couples, families, work groups, or organizations—have a proclivity towards either *strategic* or *intimate* ways of approaching the world. There is a tendency in many always to go to the one approach that they are most skilled at, attracted to, understand best, and are more comfortable with. Often, they don't even know that other possibilities exist and, if they do, they have little interest in exploring them. In our training, we teach practitioners to view relationships through both of these lenses, and to consider them as complicated *polarities.*

Polarities can be defined simply as sets of interdependent opposites, like the straightforward concepts of hot/cold, soft/hard, fast/slow; or the more complicated optimist/pessimist, introvert/extrovert. But once we get past the simple ones, we find that there may be many *opposites* attached to a pole. Take the concept of love for example. If you were randomly asking people to identify the opposite, many would automatically say hate, reflecting the black/white way we often see things. But the famous political activist and holocaust survivor, Elie Wiesel, held a more expansive view and stated, "The opposite of love is not hate. It's indifference" (1986). So, if we broaden our repertoire of love's polarity, we might possibly include dislike, animosity, antagonism, disgust, repulsion, loathing, abhorrence, hostility, or rancor.

Now, if we lead a full life, we might not be as prone to polarizing and have a multiplicity of poles, with an in-between range as well—for example, being able to view the world from both an optimistic or pessimistic perspective; and, at times, a mixture of both. But if we respond to situations with only one outlook, then our possibilities for engaging the world are diminished. Our ability to see and respond is influenced, not only by our personal history and family of origin, but also by the institutions of country, church, school, and work where we grow and live. Much of individual psychotherapy focuses on the origins of the client's diminished capacity to see, hear, and respond.

Fritz Perls (1969) was interested in polarities, especially that which he labeled *top dog/underdog*. The top dog was comprised of the "shoulds," i.e., the rules of the world, while the underdog reflected the individual's "wants," the more primitive, self-centered and emotionally-driven side. Perls not only looked at the composition of each pole but, more importantly, at the relationship that existed between them.

In a new relationship, our attraction is often directed toward the pole representing qualities that we have minimally developed in ourselves. When infatuated, we get to experience this characteristic without having to nurture it in ourselves, or even to be aware of it. But, as we know, the attraction to the underdeveloped pole begins in time to wear thin. This is when couples often enter therapy. For example:

136

Patti and Ivan had a pretty solid marriage. Both had definitely not married their parents. Unlike Patti's father who was frightened, avoidant of action and risk averse, Ivan was the opposite: a lover of movement, change, and excitement. He had developed what we sometimes refer to as the "I" pole, paying more attention to his wants, feelings, and interests as opposed to the experience of others. Patti, unlike Ivan's mother, was a highly socially aware person. She noticed and cared deeply about what others thought and felt. We might say she had a highly developed sense of "we."

Ivan hated having his picture taken, but would grudgingly give in during holidays and special events. He had long forgotten that he had originally been attracted to Patti's sense of relationship. In therapy, he realized that his gift of begrudgingly allowing himself to please his wife was in fact cheap and stingy. He began to learn to embrace the "we" pole and became more relationally generous. Mary also began to understand that Ivan's stubbornness and willingness to hold to an unpopular stance were part of the reason she had fallen in love with him. She began to see it as a valuable part of who he was, and to advocate more for her wants and needs instead of always putting the relationship first.

Polarities exist not just internally and in intimate systems but also in organizations, and even between cultures and countries. For instance, common organizational dilemmas have to do with the centralize/decentralize, or the strategic/intimate polarities.

Joe: *I know of an organization that prides itself on its relational culture. The CEO always has his door open, and he loves to have lunch in the cafeteria where he is on a first name basis with many of the employees. When there is a death in the corporate family, it seems that nearly everyone goes to the funeral. The executives continuously receive phone calls from head hunters who indicate that they can get them similar jobs for two or three times the salary they are currently earning. Yet rarely does anyone leave.*

There was a downside to their relational tightness. Relationship sometimes trumped skill, while creative conflict rarely occurred. If the opposite of tight relationship is loose relationship, which if developed would allow employees to leave more easily, it would open the organization to new people, ideas, and inventiveness. This did not happen, and new hires rarely survived. Also, because the intimate pole took precedence over the strategic pole, profits decreased and the organization eventually merged with another, more strategic one. At this point, many of the original executives left, depriving the new organization of much connectedness and history. Eventually, the merged company was sold and is still struggling to find a balance that works.

Often, we are aware of the well-developed and only see its upside or downside. In addition, we are not aware of our underdeveloped poles which we tend to project onto others. Much of the pain with regard to both intimate and global nature comes from acting on these unaware and disowned projections; and, at the extreme, from trying to destroy them (Melnick and E. Nevis, 2012). For example, it is easy to see that, when individuals and nations are behaving towards others in an arrogant or contemptuous manner, they are projecting their experience of being *"less than."* They do this to move from an unacceptable stance of being "one down" to a position of being "one up" (Melnick and S. Nevis, 2010). Only when both sides can own their projections is a real connection possible.

When the strategic/intimate frame is experienced as a polarity, we habitually go to the well-developed pole and dismiss and ignore the less developed one. We tend to do this over and over again, even when that choice doesn't work. As a result, we can move to an either/or stance and lose our balance—often getting the downside of both poles, rather than utilizing aspects of both (Melnick and S. Nevis, 2010).

As interveners, we need to be aware of both lenses and help our students understand how they are utilized in responding to their world. But as teachers, we need to have our students learn that the strategic/intimate perspectives are not only lenses from which to organize experience, but also consist of *skills* to be learned. We list some important ones below.

Intimacy Skills

Intimate behaviors are communications, both verbal and non-verbal, which aim to enhance connection. Our focus, however, is not on isolated behaviors, but on interactions that occur between people. Such interactions require a giver and a receiver, a sense of mutuality, and the experience of little or no hierarchical difference. *Table 2* provides examples of qualities of intimacy skills.

Table 2

INTIMACY SKILLS

The ability to:
- express interest in another that is perceived as such by the other;
- ask questions and give answers, with the goal of knowing more about each other's thoughts and feelings;
- suspend or avoid use of hierarchy during an exchange;
- commit to sustained dialogue;
- keep the interactions *fluid* through humor;
- influence the other and be influenced;
- engage in exchanges that are spontaneous and without a definite outcome in mind;
- stay focused on the here and now—the present moment;
- modulate the speed and tone of the exchange to accommodate the rhythm of others; and
- not blame one's self or others.

Strategic Skills

Strategic behaviors are actions intended to achieve a desired goal. They usually involve an exchange of influence among people who are in a hierarchical relationship. While connectedness is desired, strategic interactions override mutuality. Two people may not want the same thing, but they have an unspoken acceptance of the rules of leadership and followership. The following, in *Table 3*, are examples of the qualities of strategic skills.

140

Table 3

STRATEGIC SKILLS

The ability to:

- stay focused on a goal without being deflected by emotions;
- be abrupt, intrusive, or bold in the service of economy of time,
- make or follow an unpopular decision;
- disagree or fight for alternatives and still maintain the hierarchical alliance;
- mobilize energy in the face of disappointment;
- accept hierarchical differences relative to accountability ("As your father, I am responsible for you. You are not getting the car tonight." "Dad, it is not fair." "Perhaps not, but you are not getting the car.");
- take command or follow others who have momentarily taken command in order to form a new strategic alliance as needed;
- share only the information needed to initiate an action; and
- bear the loss of complete dialogue and the isolation or loneliness that it creates, and instead enter into an action-based, comparatively perfunctory, exchange.

In Closing

Although we have artificially broken down this chapter into intimacy and strategy, almost any interaction involves a combination of the two. Both stances incorporate skills and competencies that can be taught and learned. When systems—whether couples, families, teams, or organizations—do not have the capacity to be relational (intimate) or strategic (goal-oriented), they run the risk of getting locked into a pattern that is unresponsive to the current situation. For example, an organization that is highly strategic, when faced with a crisis, may initiate different strategic plans when the problem may, in fact, be that they have poor interpersonal relationships.

Creating the right mix of intimacy and strategy requires being aware of a number of variables including goals, time, and focus. Although a situation might require more of one than the other, they are almost always wrapped around each other—what our colleague Penny Backman has called a "seamless braid." When to move from connection to action and back to connection requires a sense of the aesthetics of the situation.

10

POWER, HIERARCHY, AND LEADERSHIP

Sonia: *I was thinking that the higher up we are in the hierarchy, the more power we have. Power allows me to make my own decisions. I don't have to wait. I get to decide what we have to do.*[19]

Joe: *With families, the relational hierarchy is always shifting, primarily in response to the developmental stages of the children. In organizations, by way of contrast, the power shifts are often more complex and less transparent.*

Sonia: *I saw a woman yesterday whose mother had made her life miserable, treating her like a friend and not a child. So many women don't know how to raise children. They don't know how to manage the hierarchy. Parents sometimes give it up; they give away the power—the power to decide and influence. And sometimes parents do the opposite; they become rigidly hierarchical.*

Joe: *When I look at organizations, it's hard to talk about hierarchy and power without focusing on the culture and the goals. Often in non-profit or volunteer organizations, the*

---

[19] There are many forms of power; the one we talk about often is positional power. There are a number of other forms of power such as coalitional power, wherein followers or children band together to thwart the power of positional leaders. This dynamic is sometimes true in families and organizations. That's why it is difficult to talk about hierarchy without also talking about power.

hierarchical relationship and the ability to influence are fuzzy.[20] *In others, like military organizations or surgical units, hierarchy and power tend to be clearer and more fixed.*

Sonia: *We get into trouble because many of our beliefs about power and hierarchy are shaped in our childhood, and often, we are not aware of this reality.*

Joe: *Yes, when I taught this module with one of our colleagues, we talked about the differences in our growing up. She grew up a Catholic with aunts who were nuns, and she became a nurse. She was taught to respect positional power and hierarchy. As a student nurse, she was taught to exit the elevator if it was full and a physician was waiting to get in.*

My upbringing was very different. My father was anarchistic: a union man with a chip on his shoulder, and a hater of fixed hierarchy. I remember the controversy I stirred within the psychology faculty when, as a young assistant professor, I insisted that graduate students call me by my first name instead of Doctor. Times have changed. Now my granddaughter, age 8, goes to a private school where the children call their teachers and administrators by their first names and no one seems to mind. I smile.

Sonia: *I grew up with no hierarchy. My father disappeared emotionally when my mother died, and I was sent to live with a series of*

---

[20] It might be argued that this fuzziness occurs because hierarchy in most for-profit organizations is built on masculine values; whereas many non-profits are constructed on predominately female values. The latter is circular—everyone is equal—rather than with rungs of authority (Curran, K., 2015).

Joe: *families as an outsider. Because I was temporary, I didn't have to conform or rebel. My parents had a disrespect for hierarchy, so I didn't have to rebel against them. Instead, I rebelled against others. Still, when I see a hierarchy that is rigid, my belly tightens up and my adolescent self reemerges.*

Sonia: *I remember when we invited the leadership group of a police department to spend a day with us as clients, so our students could practice our model.[21] The chief walked in with his flip chart and markers. With barely a hello, he ignored me and our students and began organizing the day. He said nothing to me. He jumped right over me and started taking over the class. I went up to him and explained that we were similar—that outside, he was the chief and people needed to follow him—but that inside at GISC, I was higher than the police chief for the moment. I had to take my power. I needed to be higher than the chief for all our sakes, including the police and students, in order to have a good experience. Otherwise, no one would listen to me. Luckily, he smiled and handed me the marker, giving me permission to be the leader.[22]*

Joe: *You took your power, and he allowed you to take it and to lead. Sometimes you have to take a risk in order to create followership.*

---

[21] In our program, Applying the Cape Cod Model (CCM) to Organizations, we invite leadership teams of organizations to receive a free day of consultation from our students.

[22] At the end of the session, the chief gifted Sonia with a police hat that she placed in the rear window of her car. This allowed her to avoid any traffic tickets on Cape Cod!

Sonia: *Normally, as a consultant, coach, or therapist, one of my first tasks is to get the group to allow me to be the temporary leader. Usually I speak to the leader off line, prior to the first meeting, in order to create enough trust for him or her to let me lead. But this wasn't true in the case of the police chief. We were all strangers to each other. If it is done well, you become aligned with the top of the hierarchy; if you don't shame them, they will support your work.*

Joe: *And it isn't just that you need to get the leader to get to follow you. I remember when working with a group of litigators, one of the younger lawyers opened up a newspaper and started reading it just as I began to talk. At first, I was startled. Then I began walking around the room continuing to talk. When I got to him I firmly took the newspaper, folded it up, and placed it next to him. I didn't want to fight with him or humiliate him. I said nothing, and neither did anyone else. We were all fine after that.*

Sonia: *Yes, there is often a magic moment when the hierarchy and power relationship shift. It is often non-verbal.*

Joe: *I have a number of clients, abused as children, who have told me of a moment when they stood tall and looked the parental abuser in the eye as they were being hit. Surprised, the abuser stopped, walked away, and never attempted physically to harm them again.*

Power and Leadership

Historically in Western society, leaders were leaders and followers were followers. The roles were clear and fixed, making it nearly impossible to move up the ladder. Leadership was often an accident of birth, such as in churches and monarchies. Power, the ability to influence relationships and outcomes—i.e., doing almost whatever we wanted to do and telling others what to do—rested almost solely with the leaders. This unbalanced distribution of power in the USA changed radically as a result of events of World War II.[23]

The profound cultural shift was ignited by a number of converging factors. First, the war forced different classes, races, and religions to intermingle in ways that otherwise never would have happened. On the front lines, one's power was based less on wealth and status and more on rank and, in principle, competence. Not only were these soldiers forced to live, eat, and fight together, thus creating new relationships, but they were facing life-changing experiences in a much more complex environment. They were no longer members of small, largely homogeneous clans but instead citizens of the world. Power relationships were no longer fixed at birth.[24] People had real life experiences

---

[23] We do not wish to oversimplify this shift. For example, for generations, immigrants have entered the United States and rather than simply "melting" have challenged the hierarchical structure and beliefs.

[24] There were other important changes. Rather than everything being handed down from one generation to the next, resulting in a form of cultural stagnation, people began to learn more from each other as subcultures mingled and interacted. Of specific interest is that elders were learning more from those who were younger. As a result, people experienced more personal power.

with shifting power and returned from war knowing a good deal about the process of influencing. Also, because of special post-war governmental funding for veterans, many who would never have thought of attending college were able to do so without paying. Thus, many were able to earn a college degree, an important component for entering the "leadership club."

During that time, too, with the men off to war, women not only took over managing home and family but also worked in defense plants, frequently side by side with men. Both genders were forced to relate to each other every day around work, and the women more than held their own. The image of *Rosie the Riveter* is still etched proudly in the American psyche.

Immediately after the war, with veterans returning to reclaim jobs, women were told to pack up, go home, and return to the kitchen. Feminist writers like Betty Friedan understood that once you get a taste of power and influence, it is hard to go back to always being a powerless follower. The feminists said that women could not be treated in this fashion. A growing number of men who had witnessed women's competence agreed with them, and a whole movement started that wasn't limited to just women.

Many of the returning veterans were African Americans who, having experienced a world very different from their home, were no longer willing to assent quickly to what they were expected to be. The movement that challenged and changed traditional power relationships reached a pinnacle when Barack Obama was elected the first African-American president of the United States. Those relationships expanded to include many minority groups, including religious, immigrants, and those with different sexual orientations. All of these groups, even the more successful ones, continue to fight for their rightful place.

As a result of this cultural shift, the leadership pool

increased, as did the complexity in the relationship between leaders and followers. Followers now had more resources and options, including the power of the collective. They were able to say a strong no. The labor movement is a well-known example of this shift. At the beginning, there were many violent armed conflicts between management and labor in their struggles over power and influence. As the struggles continued, it became clear that neither could tell the other what to do. The leaders' ability to get things done was profoundly related to their relationship with their followers. Both groups needed each other. They needed to talk, agree, disagree, and cooperate if the organization was to reach its potential. People began to understand that working together well was the answer.

The same trend was happening in the home. Children were no longer willing to be "seen and not heard." Parents were talking more to their children and, more importantly, listening and being influenced by what they had to say. Like organizational leaders, parents were realizing that the old ways of managing power and influence no longer worked. As in any leader/follower relationship, too much of children's good energy gets wasted if they are not heard.

When we experience ourselves as being respected for what we can do, wish to do, see, and notice, then tremendous potential is unleashed in the family, organization, or culture. Relationships where people are able to impact each other lead to better outcomes. We all must work together for the most good to occur. On the other hand, when any group becomes a permanent underclass, with little or no impact, everyone loses. The underclass either resists or withdraws as their energy and commitment diminish.

In this age of complexity and multiple realities, it is harder to bring people together. With multiple stakeholders and more complex power dynamics, the chances of agreeing on a common goal are more difficult than before. Competent leaders must understand that most people are doing the best they can, and that resistance and opposition must be encountered respectfully. Leaders must be optimistic, embodying a trust that things will continue to get better.

To be empowered means to be able to choose between options, to move towards the chosen object with grace, and to accept the consequences of one's actions. Thus, a sense of empowerment goes hand in hand with a sense of responsibility for one's actions. Choices are made with an equally grounded ownership of what was given up as well as what was chosen.

Be that as it may, power differentials of a consistent and relatively fixed manner do exist in many intimate systems. Furthermore, as an individual matures through life experience, the pendulum of power will swing more and more to his or her side of the boundary.

Well-used power generates a rich and protected interactive culture in which the less mature can learn and grow. Effective parents are thus able to provide the protection, consistency, and safety necessary for the child to develop unencumbered by adult-like concerns and issues. Similarly, strong teachers take responsibility for the tutelage of the student, creating a milieu in which modeling and the introjection of ideas and values can occur. Lastly, the able therapist creates a setting and atmosphere in which the client can ultimately integrate more negative aspects of self that had previously been disowned and rejected (Melnick and S. Nevis, 1998, p. 43).

Hierarchy

We are predisposed to order our world, to have certain experiences stand out in relation to others. Gestalt psychologists have described this process as *figure/ground*. If it were not for this hard wiring, our lives would be unstructured and totally chaotic. Children learn that some are prettier, smarter, funnier, more sensitive, or meaner than others. The relational tension in hierarchies is of extreme importance. Some tend to be fluid like children choosing sides for a game. Others tend to be more fixed and structured, like that of a king and his subjects or many Western, for-profit organizations.

Hierarchy in Peer Relationships

Many, if not most, relationships in the world consist of peers: neighbors, friends, and people with whom we go to school or to houses of worship. Every relationship is different, and we need to know how to connect in each one. To do this, we must learn a large set of skills to manage differences.

Peer relationships are different from hierarchical ones and, in many ways, more complex. The roles are more fluid and less predetermined and defined. When you are peers, you both share the responsibility of knowing what is needed, i.e., what is important, and what you are expecting from each other at any moment. Sometimes decisions and actions are managed jointly; we both decide together as equals. At other times, the relationship is more hierarchical. We both decide that one has more of a right to tell the other what to do. Our decision might be based on competence, or what we might term *expert* power. For example, one might be the better cook, money manager, or decorator. Sometimes the greater interest will win. And sometimes we might just flip a coin. Here is a case example:

Jan and Bill had always had a marriage of equals. They had always both worked and shared the financial and household duties. They also had independent lives. This balance changed when Jan decided to join Bill in his love for sailboat racing. At first, she just hung around and watched. She noticed that many of the two-person teams consisted of committed couples. She also noticed that when they docked their boats at the end of a race, these couples often did not look happy or pleased with each other. Being therapists and inquisitive by nature, Jan and Bill started talking to them and found that many struggled over how to decide matters on the boat. Both decided that, when they were on the boat, Bill would be the captain and Jan would be the crew. His word would be law, and if she had any issues, they would be discussed after the race. They did quite well competing and never had a fight.

In this case, there is hierarchy because both people are not on an equal plane. But overall the relational hierarchy is fluid, situational, and decided by both. In the sailing context, Jan and Bill had to figure out who was best equipped to lead, how to make a decision together, and how to give in when one thought he or she was right.

Hierarchy and Leadership

Many leaders believe that they have the power to make things happen, and that this is their essential role. Yet leading is more complex than that. What they frequently do not know is that the first task of a leader is to gain the *trust* of their subordinates. Until this happens, the work of leading cannot take place. And there has to be a willingness and ability of the leader to lead. Otherwise, there can easily be disarray and confusion.

When the leadership hierarchy is fixed or

permanent, such as parent to child, managing life's tasks may be clearer, but not necessarily easier. In an organization with boss/subordinate relationships, the hierarchy is less fixed, more of a social contract, but still hierarchical in that the freedom of subordinates is limited if they wish to keep their jobs or rise in the organization. One of the leader's primary functions is to create roles and responsibilities—the relational contract. Done well, expectations are clarified, resistances worked through, actions agreed upon, uncertainty diminished, and safety created. Here are some other leadership responsibilities:

- Leaders have more of the responsibility for creating a good relationship by managing inclusion and engagement. Along with this responsibility comes the right to tell the followers what to do. The followers are left with the choice of how to respond.
- Leaders are more responsible for establishing rules, creating a safe culture, being highly aware of what is going on with the people they are guiding, and knowing how they impact them. For example, in families, parents have to create safety by speaking out and getting feedback from their children.
- Because leaders have greater influence, they have the added responsibility of getting the job done and overseeing the relationship, i.e., of getting their followers to listen and do what they, the leaders, want. This is not as easy as it sounds. Being permanently *one down* in a relationship is difficult for most of us. So even when done well, resentment can be present. Few of us like to be told what to do. "Who are you to be telling me what to do? Who are you to think you know me?"
- Competent leaders know that influence doesn't automatically come from being in control; it comes from creating trust—and not just a one-way kind,

from follower to leader. Trust must go both ways. Leaders also must trust their followers. Effective leaders also know how to repair trust when it is frayed or fractured, because in any evolving relationship the breaking of trust is common.[25]

Sonia: *The leader has to make connections with the team before she tells them what they need to do. I have had a number of experiences in which the leader is not leading. Have you ever had that experience?*

Joe: *Yes, lots of leaders don't know how to lead.*

Sonia: *Can you remember situations when you have struggled with leading?*

Joe: *Yes. I always saw myself as a collaborative leader and, because of my past and beliefs, I was always anti-hierarchy. In time, I discovered that I wasn't as collaborative as I thought. Rather than tell people what I wanted, I wanted them to do it without having to tell them. They needed to figure it out by watching me. After a number of these experiences, I began to realize that I have a responsibility to speak my wants, and to determine the pace. Otherwise I confuse people.*

Sonia: *I've never put into words what I'm trying to*

---

[25] Since the birth of psychotherapy, there has been confusion regarding the hierarchical relationship between client and therapist. Are we in service to them or are we in charge? Are we the knowable expert or a slightly enlightened fellow traveler? And there is still confusion around defining this complex relationship. Most of us do not have the language to define the quick, complex, back and forth movement between intimacy and strategy necessary for therapy (and nearly all hierarchical relationships) to move forward.

say. If we are going to train leaders, it is at a higher level. I can make a good connection with people but, as a consultant, I can't take the process over from leaders or it will shame them—even though many leaders say, "You take it over, I'll just watch." But watching me lead isn't as helpful as it seems because leaders will not be getting something for themselves, and they will be one-upped by us.

Joe: *How do leaders get people to follow them? Some leaders are so hierarchical that they shut people off, and some are so collaborative that the followers think that the leader is a friend.*

Sonia: *It would be great if leaders could ask, "How am I doing?" like Mayor Koch used to do with the residents of New York City.*

Hierarchy and Power

It is hard to describe and understand hierarchy without discussing the concept of *power*. As we mentioned above, in most well-functioning families, *power—the ability to influence and manage differences*—rests primarily with the parents. They have more relational power; the children less. In fact, it is often the case that families in trouble are misaligned and confused regarding how hierarchy and power are managed.

Certainly, the parent/child dynamic and how to manage it should be clear; the parent is always the parent and the child the child. The parent's primary job is to lead, and the child's is to follow. As psychotherapists, we noticed that when this hierarchy was not clear and respected, the family was often in for a tough time. We became reflexively nervous when we were with families in which a child functioned more as an adult than the parents (what therapists refer to as the "parentified child"), or when parents described themselves as being *friends* with their young offspring.

We are now in an era of complexity, during which time the forms of hierarchical power have shifted and become more fluid and collaborative. The more involvement people have in an organization, the better the end result. We understand now that power does not reside solely in the individual. *All power is relational.* Even an assigned or elected leader (such as the President of the United States), a biological leader (such as a parent), or the sole owner of a company does not have power alone. Just try this. Ask any competent leaders you know if they have power. Inevitably, they will look at you and say, "Absolutely not!" or, if they know you well, "What? Are you crazy?"

Then who does have power? The relationship has. It is only when people are pulling together—whether on the family system level (parents and children), the organizational level (leaders and followers), the microcosmic governmental level (elected representatives), or the ultra-macrocosmic, global level (nation to nation)—that goals are reached, important work gets done, and people are satisfied and happier. When they do not pull together, they create a stalemate. Or, as the current term applied to the US Congress indicates, the result is *gridlock. Competent leaders know that power, in its essence, involves the ability to be relationally influential.* They know when to be more authoritarian, when to be collaborative, when to challenge, when to give in, when to hold their ground, when to acknowledge that they have made a mistake, and when to say "I'm sorry."

In the Cape Cod Training Program, we teach leaders—old and new—to get acquainted with their subordinates in specific ways: by supporting their asking questions and then answering them; by acknowledging when something is well done; and by expressing disappointment when work is not accomplished. This approach results in a creative and productive workforce, where the power of the leader is accepted.

> **Joe:** *For many years, I consulted to surgical residents of a medical center to help teach them how to be less authoritarian and more relational. An operating room is not much different from a military environment or a police station, in that the hierarchy is clear and absolute as these groups face life and death situations. Surgeons are known to speak angrily and sometimes abusively to anyone on their team whom they see as too slow or incompetent. Over the years, I got to know who the favorite surgeons were. They were not the few mild-mannered, collaborative ones. Instead they were members of the angry group, for the residents believed that sometimes saving a patient required quick, uncensored action. What stood out among these favorite doctors was that they always located the resident for a coffee or beer afterwards to process the experience and repair the relationship.*[26]

---

[26] Entailed here is a blend of what we have called *strategic* and *intimate* (detailed above). Such a situation can also be described in terms of *communal* (feminine) versus *agenic* (masculine). When there is a polarization towards one or the other (such as in the communal "occupy movement" in the United States at the expense of the agenic), little happens. The best solution is to combine and embody the best of both ways of being, as those impactful physicians did.

Working Relationships

Consultants and Coaches

We were attracting not only clinicians to our programs, but also coaches and organizational consultants. In addition to having similar relational dynamics as clinicians do in managing hierarchies, these professionals had to deal with the power/hierarchical equation that exists in all institutions. While many were employed by organizations internally, others were contracted as external consultants or coaches. So even when working just with individuals (as in most coaching situations), they were still paid by and responsible to the organization, resulting in an intricate interplay of hierarchical relationships.

Because of this complexity, one of the coach's and consultant's first tasks is to define the parameters of this relationship, and to get a clear agreement regarding the power dynamics. And, of course, even when there is a *clear* contract, the clarity often gets diminished or whittled away over time. Once the consultant or coach gets hierarchical recognition, and the client places him/herself in the role of learner, then both can begin to move forward toward achieving their agreed upon goals (Melnick and Nevis, 1987).

The Academy Award winning film, *The King's Speech*, can be viewed as a good example of a consultant (an non-traditional speech therapist) working with a client. In this unique instance, the client, the King of England seeking help for his stammer, is dramatically above the consultant socially, financially, and culturally. The consultant works consistently to establish a hierarchical relationship, so that the King will follow him. He uses many of the strategies listed above. Occasionally, when his interventions are off the mark and the King gets angry, and even refuses to continue,

158

the consultant relies on intimacy skills to repair the relationship. As anyone who has seen the film can attest, the King learns, after many trials and tribulations, to give a speech without stuttering, and the two men forge a relationship that endures beyond the original contract.

Teaching Leaders, Coaches, and Consultants

We teach leaders, coaches, and consultants, not just by lecturing and having them practice, but also by living out the model. They come to us in order to learn how to create an organizational culture in which their work force will listen and follow them. They understand that, as participants in our program, they are the followers and we the leaders. They notice not only what we say about leader/follower dynamics, but how we live it in our work with them. They watch how we create trust so that they will let us be their teachers. They don't just listen to us talking about the importance of making connections; they experience it.

We teach our students to:

- establish a level of trust before entering into the work, in part by explaining what needs to be done, and what the goals are;
- recognize a rhythm to intimacy and strategy (the Cycle of Experience)—of first connecting and then commanding, of first relating and then acting;
- turn from an intimate to a strategic stance to get the work done and then to a more intimate stance in order to complete a meeting; and
- value the strategic and intimate modes of relationship, i.e., when to be intimate (peer-like), and when to be strategic (hierarchical).

159

Once our students begin to assimilate these principles, they find themselves leading in a more skilled way.

Our Hierarchical Beliefs and Interventions

We all carry within us a set of predispositions that impact which hierarchical patterns we see, and which keep us interested. And, of course, there is our belief as to which forms work best and which skills are necessary. The more we are aware of these biases or predispositions, the more we are able to sit back and see (see chapter 12). We list below our beliefs concerning hierarchical systems below followed by specific *tips* for creating a more functional, productive, and *evolving* hierarchical relationship.

Table 4

OUR BELIEFS

- Generally, it is in the nature of any social or work group for hierarchy to occur. People are compelled to organize into patterned, redundant ways of forming a status ladder.
- Patterns and ways of relating are different in every family or organization. To look for a normal one or a *right* one with expected sequences is naïve and creates difficulties.
- The first task of a consultant is to join the system. To join, you must first be aware of how the power-related hierarchy is being managed. You need to join through the leader.
- Most of us tend to have specific reactions to authority that are deeply ingrained. We also have specific values and beliefs around influencing. It is important to be aware of our values and reactions to different forms of authority.
- Flexibility is necessary. A rigid, narrow leader/follower hierarchy cannot adjust to changes in context.
- Hierarchy, when well-managed, leads to creativity which is essential for development.
- Individuals become increasingly less regulated in direct proportion to the number of malfunctioning hierarchies of which they are a part.

Table 5

**TIPS FOR WORKING WITH
HIERARCHICAL GROUPS**

- Remember that a leader has multiple tasks, i.e., monitoring the process of the group and individuals as well as setting the goals of the meeting.
- Be aware of how the hierarchy is maintained and diminished.
- When tracking the flow of power, notice patterns that alter hierarchy. They can be subtle.
- Interventions directed to the leader should be about the process of the entire system.
- Make (nearly) every intervention a systemic one.
- A system with a single leader at times looks like there is a vacancy. (The single leader has no one to turn to on his or her level.) Often a group member will temporarily occupy the vacancy. Watch for how this occurrence impacts the hierarchical process. Vacancies may be out of the awareness of the system.
- As a consultant, gracefully join the leader and support the hierarchy. In that case you are making a subsystem out of the leader and you. Notice how you enter that subsystem.
- Look out for cross-hierarchical coalitions. This is when someone at one level of hierarchy consistently forms a coalition with a member at another level.
- Pay attention to your stance toward hierarchical organizations.
- Look for patterns, not attitudes, of the leader.
- When confronted with resistance/push-back (multiple realities), lean in and get interested rather than defensive.
- Remember that every hierarchical organization is cultural, contextual, and goal-dependent.
- When working with two or more people, pay

162

attention to the development of every subsystem.
- To first see problems with leadership is natural. So take time to look for the patterns in the system (not attributes or habits in the leader) that subtly shift, alter, maintain, or strengthen the hierarchy.
- Working with a group that has a designated leader creates added complexity for a consultant or therapist. There is a fixed hierarchical structure that must be respected, though often issues in this structural arrangement prevent the group (or family) from reaching its potential.

Before ending this section, we should mention that more and more consultants are being asked to work with non-traditional groups, teams, and organizations. These groups are set up to be collaborative, self-organizing, of short-term duration, and non-hierarchical, with no assigned leader. In these situations, in which power and influence are emergent, the intervener's work is still the same. It is to assist the group to work effectively, creatively, and productively by watching for patterns of behaviors and determining whether they support the work of the group or diminish its effectiveness.

In Closing

Effective leaders, coaches, therapists, and consultants know how to establish trust and get respect—what we call *intimacy*; and how to get others to follow in order to reach goals—what we call *strategy*. In the Cape Cod Model, we establish trust by first articulating the strengths that individuals and groups already have. Individuals often do not know their own strengths, and neither do teams and groups. The articulation of strengths begins a process of connecting with individuals and the group. You are seeing and hearing them, interested in them, and telling them about something they are doing—a competency—that has often been forgotten, overlooked, or undervalued.

We underscore that the Gestalt concept known as the *Paradoxical Theory of Change* states that telling people what they actually are *doing* will go further toward promoting change than telling them what they should do differently. Learning is strong when people become aware of their actions. It helps create trust, and only when trust is established does teaching become possible. It is then that the processes essential for optimal functioning of a person or a group can be taught. This sequence of teaching—first bringing strengths into awareness, and only then bringing the underdeveloped aspects of the individual or a group into awareness—is an important part of the Cape Cod Model.

SECTION THREE

HOW WE TEACH:

INTERVENER SKILLS

INTRODUCTION

How We Teach

Our model has been built from our experiences. We would get an idea, try it out, see if it held up in practice, and determine if it might possibly fit into our developing model. By "fit," we don't mean like pieces in a puzzle. When you introduce something into a system, even a theoretical one, everything changes.

The puzzle is more than three-dimensional. It's as if it is alive, constantly changing and developing, becoming both simpler and more complex. Each time an idea was entertained, whether it ended up being included or not, the total model changed. Each time we taught a concept, it came out a little different. And our students were a big part of this process. They were delighted to be able to be an active part of growing our theory. Our program is an immersion experience, in which the theory is lived every moment. Although the stated goals are about skill-building, for many the program becomes much more. Let us explain.

Most of us can easily remember times in school when we asked a question and ended up feeling stupid. And even when someone else was being shamed for asking, we still felt ourselves shrinking back. In these classes, we became more interested in not getting things wrong than in taking risks and learning something new. Unlike these early memories, we want to provide our participants with a very different experience. We want to create a maximally supportive learning environment, where *not knowing things* is a benefit, where being awkward is celebrated as essential to new learning, and where all are in charge of their own development.

Our model builds trust by focusing on our experiences with others:

- How we begin.
- How we engage.
- How we share our experiences.
- How we disengage.

We teach it in a step-by-step progression. It is a scaffolding process, with each experience added one at a time. We place a premium on practicing the different steps, much like a young pianist learns to play her scales until they become habit. As steps are practiced and learned, new ones are added regularly.

From the beginning, we understood that we had to practice what we preached. All too often, we entered organizations that had well thought out vision and mission statements, catchy slogans, and rules of conduct that were not practiced by the leaders. We understood that subordinates, whether children, students, or line staff, pay much more attention to how their leaders behave toward them and each other than to their spoken or written words. Below is an example of how an effort to be strategic and hierarchical ignored the underlying relational dysfunction of the system.

> **Joe:** *A group of physicians I was working with were angry and embarrassed by how a senior member was treating staff and patients. The physician leader called me in to help the executive committee decide what to do. He believed that the issue could be resolved by hiring a lawyer to create a code of conduct, including punishment, to which everyone would agree. He wanted to know what I thought.*
>
> *Prior to calling me, the leader had only had one casual conversation with the other physicians.*

As I discovered in my interview process, he had no idea of how angry and critical the physicians were of his inaction. The leader did not see the problem as organizational or relational, but due to a lack of rules. The problem would be solved by having an outsider create them. In fact, the executive committee had planned to impose this set of rules without consulting their partners, including the one with whom they were angry.

I asked the leader if he would be willing to suspend, demote, or possibly fire the problematic partner. He gave a quick, nervous NO. Not just the leader, but the entire group was conflict averse and did not understand that if they wished for a better organization, they had to learn to deal with their differences, especially ones related to hierarchy. They also needed to learn that they were treating their offending partner in the same way he was treating others, dismissively and arbitrarily.[27]

In our work, we understood that we needed to treat our students the same way we were asking them to treat each other. We could not say, "This is how you talk to people," while talking differently to them. If we had, we would have lost all trust and credibility. As a faculty, we had been teaching and living this way for so long— it was so much a part of who we collectively were—that we had never identified it. Probably at its core was the *golden rule* of treating others as we wish to be treated.[28]

---

[27] This inability or unwillingness for physicians to confront their peers is one of the cultural issues that has negatively impacted medical care in the USA.

[28] Not surprising, research suggests that for many, emotional well-being rests on your ability to treat yourself as well as you treat others; what theorists call "self-compassion" (Weir, 2011). According to Neff (2011), self-compassion consists of

But once we began to pay attention, we realized that the golden rule was too simple, too general to describe what we did. We had to break it down into smaller pieces, a set of skills that could be applied to different phases of the Cycle and could be learned by our participants. We eventually grouped them into the following categories.

- Creating trust: How to create and maintain it. This involves our being *present* in an authentic way.
- Seeing a system: How to notice what is going on *between* individuals and within the system as a *whole*.
- Intervening: How to give feedback in a respectful and impactful way, and how to work with *resistance and create experiments*.
- Ending well: How to finish in a way so that the learning *sticks*.

Having learned these skills, our students leave as better leaders, coaches, consultants, and therapists. What they have mastered has an impact far beyond their professional lives. They have learned a way of being; a way of seeing, speaking and doing. Above all while living in a learning community, they have developed new *ways of relating* that have profoundly changed how they live in the world.

---

three components: increased awareness, viewing experience through a broad lens, and minimizing judgments.

11

CREATING TRUST

It is always our first task to develop trust between our students and ourselves.[29] Sometimes we can do it quickly, but more often it takes time. In fact, if trust develops too quickly, we become a little concerned. Quick trust, like infatuation, seldom has a long shelf-life. When relationships fail or meetings don't work, it is often because people do not know how to establish and maintain trust. In our professional roles, there are established practices to which most of us conform. We pay attention to trust building even before the first meeting by placing our diplomas, licenses, and affiliations on our office walls. In addition, many of us have web pages that introduce ourselves even before we meet.

We all learn quickly to pay attention to how we dress, to show up on time, and to speak with confidence and empathy. Coming highly recommended, or having an outstanding resume certainly helps our clients have

---

[29] The diminishment of trust in others is well documented in society. For example, only one-third of Americans say most people can be trusted. Furthermore, some researchers say that a person's trust level is set in their mid-twenties and is unlikely to change. Also, on many occasions we can't trust our senses, particularly what we say, see, and hear. This research varies from the semi-humorous, such as the popular experiment in which people are given a task to watch a group bounce a ball back and forth. Many do not see a person dressed in a gorilla suit move slowly through the group. Or on a more serious note, there is much research that questions the ability of eye-witnesses to accurately remember events (*Maine Sunday Telegram*, 2013).

some initial faith in our competence. But they don't know us, and if they are smart, they won't easily trust a stranger—no matter who recommended us, or what our professional credentials look like. If they are smart, they will wait to experience being with us.

The way many change agents create initial trust is by first asking their clients to tell them what the problem is, what is wrong. This approach seems normal for most of us, like when we get sick and go to a doctor. The belief is that something is amiss or the client wouldn't be calling us in the first place, or that by first having them discuss their dilemmas and then responding empathetically and with understanding, most people will relax. But there is a downside to creating an initial pattern, in which the client and professional focus on understanding the problem and figuring out what to do about it. It often ignores the client's competencies and creates a power dynamic in which the intervener is seen as having the solution to often-complex issues. And whatever relief clients might receive by unburdening themselves to a compassionate stranger is offset by the reinforcement of their belief that they are unable to manage their problems.

In our model, we build trust differently. Trust building is relational and not one-way. For example, as described below, responding relationally to a question provides an entry to trust-building, not just with the questioner but with the entire group. Because trust building is two-way, we also have to learn to trust our students, just as leaders must learn to trust their followers. We must trust:

- their intention, and the questions they are asking,
- that they really want to know, and
- that they are not just teasing or ambushing us.

The primary way we create trust is by focusing on

competence. We are interested in what our clients do well. (We talk about this at length later.) We also see trust building as an ongoing process, slow to create, usually difficult to grow and maintain, and always relational. Building trust takes work, and it takes skill. We work hard to create it in our program and we do it in a number of ways. One of the most important is how we *show up*, and how we initially connect and engage with our clients. This involves what Gestaltists call *presence,* the ability to use ourselves as a tool or instrument (what we call *use of self*) for inspiring growth and connection.

Establishing Presence

What is presence? Here is Edwin Nevis's (1987) viewpoint:

> The ways in which ideas are expressed, the quality of energy displayed, and the perceived values of an individual all contribute to presence. Presence is not manufactured; it is something everyone displays at all times, whether one is aware of what others respond to or not. However, presence is most powerful when it embodies a compelling model or theory of learning (p. 75).

Sonia reminisces about how she became aware of her presence and its impact on others.

> **Sonia:** *When we were talking about Ed's doing his presentation on presence, it triggered many memories, some connected with my early days with Fritz Perls. And there's something about wanting to tell these stories so that they can remain for future generations and not be lost;*

there's so much to tell. So, I thought of two things—one thing to tell you, and one thing to try; an exercise that Fritz gave us and you can do it.

One thing that made a huge difference in my being able to be present occurred while watching video tapes of therapy sessions. It was in Esalen and Fritz would work in the morning with people, and we would go over the films in the evening session. As I was watching one film, I saw myself a lot from the back. That was so startling to me that it made a shift. I absolutely gave up. I realized that I was powerless to influence what you're going to see about me, and what you're going to like and not like. In that moment—I can still remember the sensation—I thought, "It doesn't matter what I want; I can't control what you see. It's useless. I just have to do what I do, and I have to like what I like, and I have to be what I am." And I think that was probably the beginning of my understanding of presence and knowing, for instance, that when I want to be heard, I need to do something different from when I don't want to be heard. Several of you have mentioned that presence means you need to be heard. NO! Presence means you decide when you want to do something, when you want to be heard, when you want to be . . . whatever.

But what I really wanted to tell you was the exercise that Fritz once gave us that made a huge difference to my presence and, I believe, to a lot of others' presence. The exercise is called "The Village Idiot." (We are aware that today, such appellation is not acceptable; we include it to reflect experience back then, which had a profound effect on Sonia's sense of her personal presence).

It is the most freeing thing. There's a village

174

idiot in every one of us, and we're always afraid for it to come out. Many of the things we do are idiotic, and once I learned that there's no harm in being an idiot, life became easier.

I grew up being a silent person for good reasons. I didn't want to be seen. I didn't want to be heard. And that was that. Fritz taught me that I have a choice. At any given moment, I can sit and not say anything, or I can put myself out there; I learned how to do it.

If you're trying to hide parts of yourself, you will be tight and your presence will be diminished. But there are times when this is just what's needed, okay? And if we can become friendly with all parts of ourselves, we've got presence for whatever is required in the moment. And that's my understanding of presence, and it is very freeing. If you can really be free, you can be present.

We return again to E. Nevis's (1987) notions on presence:

The first task of a Gestalt intervener involves presenting our self in such a way that interest and trust get generated in the client. Presence can be defined in many ways. A common definition is that it is the sum of who we are, (some might say our essence), including our age, gender, sexual orientation, and physical characteristics. Some also include our style, i.e., how we move, speak, dress, our emotional tone, and general manner, and what naturally grabs our curiosity (p. 70).

As Sonia described above, presence includes our ability to be *present* in the here and now. When we are present, we are more energized than when we are operating out of a more habitual way of being. There is an openness to nuances, with a greater potential for response. The more aware and friendlier we are with all parts of ourselves, the greater our potential to have a fuller presence. And we are not just talking about our kindness and generosity but also our gullibility, vindictiveness, selfishness, and passivity. The greater the congruence of our beliefs concerning human nature, i.e., what creates change and our expression of ourselves, the greater our presence and, thus, the greater our ability to impact others.

Our potential impact expands as our awareness, range, and ability to use different parts of ourselves increases. Do we have a wide range of skills to create trust, engage, make contact, and influence? Are we self-aware, able to notice patterns, intervene in a balanced way? Are we flexible in terms of what parts of ourselves we use in responding to situations?

Jane, a petite and mild-mannered organizational consultant, was about to begin working with a group of high-powered male executives who were all former athletes. She asked her male mentor if he would join her as a support. He refused to do so, saying that given his gender and white hair she would be perceived as the junior consultant. Instead, he suggested that she arrive, slightly late, pick out the biggest man in the group, walk up to him and say, "Excuse me, you are sitting in my chair." She did so and was surprised when he rose and went to another one. From that point on, she had little trouble in impacting this group.

So, again, what is presence?

- It is not about charisma or character, but about essence.
- It is about the ability to respond to new situations.
- It is about how you show up—how you carry yourself from situation to situation—how you sit, stand, laugh, etc.
- It is about what you easily bring forward and what you put forward.
- It involves the underlying assumptions about how you influence people—facts, relationships, and empathy.
- It is about self-awareness, i.e., the ability to look around.
- It incorporates skills for impacting others. You need a wide range of skills to make contact.
- It is also an ability to be flexible in terms of what parts of yourself you use in responding to situations.
- It is about increasing your range and using different parts of yourself.
- At its core, it is an ability to be friendly with all parts of you.

Leslie, a senior VP, complained that when she attended meetings everyone focused on her and she never had a chance to sit back and enter the conversation when she wished. A strikingly attractive woman, she wore colorful clothing, much different from the dress of the conservative organization. She also had a habit of arriving just as the meeting was about to begin, and often responded first to questions. She agreed to experiment with wearing gray, arriving early, and minimizing eye contact. She was able to do this successfully, but not without much effort. As she said, "Wearing gray is killing me." She eventually switched organizations and worked successfully for many years in the fashion industry.

We establish our presence by letting our students experience who we are, by talking to them, by being interested in what they tell us, and by answering any questions they have. We pay attention—both verbally and non-verbally—until we are connected enough to begin to tell them how we will be working together.

Our faculty at GISC has identified a number of skills that enhance presence. When we teach we sometimes have our students fill out the questionnaire below with the help of colleagues. We might have them compare their list with others, or present a case study and have them analyze it from the perspective of skills needed. Other times, we have them bring in a professional or personal situation (see *Table 6*).

Table 6

SKILLS THAT ENHANCE PRESENCE

Please circle the number that reflects your competency.

Ability to be open and receptive

1	2	3	4	5
Well-Developed			Less-Developed	

Ability to gauge and embody the appropriate amount of space for the task at hand (language, body language, tone, volume, etc.)

1	2	3	4	5
Well-Developed			Less-Developed	

Ability to stay in the here and now

1	2	3	4	5
Well-Developed			Less-Developed	

Ability to notice and be curious about physical behaviors in yourself and the other(s)

1	2	3	4	5
Well-Developed			Less-Developed	

Ability to tune in to your emotions and those of the other(s)

1	2	3	4	5
Well-Developed			Less-Developed	

Ability to separate what you observe from what you think it means

1   2   3   4   5
Well-Developed   Less-Developed

Ability to put things succinctly, clearly, and directly

1   2   3   4   5
Well-Developed   Less-Developed

Ability to embody respect, interest, and curiosity in yourself and the other(s)

1   2   3   4   5
Well-Developed   Less-Developed

Ability to use and respond to humor

1   2   3   4   5

Well-Developed   Less-Developed

Ability to be bold

1   2   3   4   5
Well-Developed   Less-Developed

Ability to be flexible

1   2   3   4   5
Well-Developed   Less-Developed

In sum, presence involves being able to transcend anxiety and be in the moment. It is about being able to notice what is happening and what to do about it. It involves good timing and pacing.[30]

Our Teaching Techniques

Asking and Responding to Questions

One of the most important skills in creating trust involves *knowing how to deal with questions.* As Rilke (1934) once put it:

> Be patient toward all that is unsolved in your heart and try to love the questions themselves like locked rooms and like books that are written in a very foreign tongue. Do not seek the answers which cannot be given you because you would not be able to live them. And the point is to live everything. Live the questions now. Perhaps you will then gradually, without noticing it, live along some distant day into the answer. (pp. 33-34)

We encourage people to ask questions, and we always answer them. We answer them fully when we can. Our main purpose in answering is not so much to offer a correct answer as to expand the question/answer conversation into a more robust dialogue. We view questions as *opportunities for engagement and trust building.* We don't answer quickly, and rarely with a fact or a yes or no. Questions are one of our best openings for dialogue.

An effective response to a question, even if it is, "I don't know," shows a willingness to engage the questioners in a variety of ways: by giving them information about ourselves, by being transparent, and by acknowledging what we don't know. And we don't

---

[30] For a different perspective on a Gestalt approach to presence, see Chidiac and Denham-Vaughan (2007, 2018).

have to stop there. We can ask others their thoughts on the question, or what they noticed was happening between us. We can turn this simple event into a group experience of trust-building. And if we don't know, we always promise to get back to them (or to the group) next time, and we do. We know that incompleteness keeps energy and anxiety high, and that completeness reduces the energy, allowing us to be present and available for the next experience. *It is this completion of an entire cycle that ultimately results in a sense of satisfaction and trust.*

Questions help us to find out if we are understood, and they aid in clearing up confusion. When we answer a question, we will often say, "Did that make sense?" "Did I answer your question?" or "Do you need to ask more?" And we listen not just to what they are saying verbally but also non-verbally. We know how to engage them, and we are always looking for resistance. We might notice a turning away or some bodily tension as the person says back, "Yes, you've answered my question." Rather than let the answer slide, we might, in turn, say, "Are you sure?" or "You seem a little hesitant. It really is okay if you didn't understand my response. Tell me where I missed you or confused you. Let's try it again."

Confusion is normal, and everyone has some responsibility to clear it up. But as teachers, it is more our responsibility. If we are willing to admit our own uncertainty and accept that of others, then a wonderful opportunity for trust-building and learning has been created. We might reply with a smile, "It's not the first time I've confused people," or "Thanks for telling me. I really can't teach, if you all don't help me like she did. Now let's take our time, because it's really important to me that you get what I'm saying."

Our students are quick to understand this way of viewing questions as representing an opportunity for trust-building and relational development. As participants first watch, and then replicate responding to questions in this different way, they are developing a tool, a way of connecting that they will use repeatedly, not just with their clients and subordinates, but in their intimate lives. And that, they tell us, makes a big difference.

We Don't Pick Favorites: There Are No Heroes or Villains

We don't pick favorites. Can you remember a time when you sat in a meeting and the leader turned to one person and said "What a great question!"? Can you remember what it feels like when someone else is the *chosen one,* making you feel invisible like a ghost in the room? From that point on, rather than having any interest in what the teacher or leader is telling you, you are instead thinking about yourself and why you were not chosen or singled out. Did you feel angry, stupid, inadequate, or just confused?

And what if you were the favorite? Did you really believe that you were so special? Did it feel good, or were you uncomfortable as you looked around at the rest of the group? In any case, by anointing one person as *better than,* the leader had probably lost you and the rest of the group or team. We also don't pick villains, singling someone out for what they are doing poorly, even if it would be *for their own good.*

> **Sonia:** *I was smart in school and loved it. I entered a new school that was academically behind in comparison to my old one. As a result, I already knew what was being taught. When the teacher would ask a question, I would put my hand up enthusiastically, because I wanted the teacher to pick me. Instead of getting picked and*

then praised for knowing, I was told, "Put your hand down. Everybody knows that you know." The teacher responded with disdain. I lost interest in the classroom, in being taught by her, and never raised my hand again in that classroom or in any other. It has been 75 years, and I can still remember that teacher's name.

Often parents pick out a child as either their favorite or as the *problem*—what clinicians call the *identified patient.* Instead of having a cohesive family that works together, the members instead pull apart. And as most clinicians know, the problem is usually not with the favorite or the problem child but with the parents. It is often a failure of leadership. Whether hero or villain or just observer, we all feel uncomfortable in situations where there is a chosen one. This is true whether a family member, student, or business associate is involved. Focusing on an individual not only impacts how we feel about our leader, but also about our peers. It results in a sense of mistrust—both in the family or group, and in the leader.

Joe: *Years ago, I worked with a charming CEO who would spend special time and lavish extra praise on new members of her leadership team. Many of the chosen ones originally felt wonderful being seen in such a glowing way.*

Luckily for the organization, the executive team was very savvy. They knew that each current favorite would be replaced by another and didn't move into competitiveness or resentment. They did not hold it against the new team member because they remembered that they had once been the favorite. Instead, they welcomed the new person into the group and were there with support when the individual fell from grace. They considered this beginning process part of the initiation ritual of becoming a member of their team. They also understood that the CEO's ability to shine a light was part of her creativity and did not hold it against her, although they did nickname her "Flavor of the Month."

No doubt we are all sensitive to being chosen or shunned. As teachers who understand this point, we never consciously pick favorites and are very careful. Any leader, teacher, or parent who consistently chooses one over the other is making trouble for the group or team. In time, the leader will have lost the ability to develop a community that can work together. We notice when our students become unbalanced when in practicum: for example, paying more attention to one of the members at the expense of the others and the group, or becoming annoyed with one. We view this loss of balance not as a mistake but as ordinary, and as a way for them to learn about *how* they have stopped seeing the family or organization as a unit, but instead as individuals. And once our students become aware of how they have stopped *seeing the system,* their behavior is usually easy to correct. Once they become aware of their own patterning, choice emerges and change is possible.

We Establish Relationships with Everyone

Our model dictates that interveners spend a significant amount of time connecting with their clients. In the past, we used to label these beginning conversations "small talk." After a while, we realized that small talk is not really small—not just something to do while getting settled in—*but an essential first step for creating trust.* This initial talking helps establish a beginning mutual interest so that we can all feel free enough to say what we need to say. Our small talk includes everyone, as we work to attend to the family or work group in a balanced way so that we are all relaxed enough to begin our work.

We Strive to Minimize Surprise

To be surprised is to have one's boundaries ruptured or circumvented. The experience of being surprised is usually accompanied by momentary immobilization and a general experience of being stymied. Physical analogies include having someone suddenly shine a light in one's face, or sneak up from behind (Melnick and S. Nevis, 1987, p. 47).

Surprises are wonderful when the object is fun, such as with games and birthdays. And a lot of teaching says that surprise keeps people's attention focused on what is happening to them. This might be true, but we believe that surprise is often not useful for learning. Surprise can make people cautious and distrustful and creates disorganization. When we are surprised, we respond without thinking. For a moment, we are thrown off balance and are psychologically naked, having temporarily lost our sense of order and form. Unless there is a great degree of established trust, surprise takes us away from our relational experience. Minimizing surprise is helpful for the creation of safety. It allows us to relax, permitting experiences to be taken in a little at a time, thus supporting slow growth.[31]

---

[31] "The individual's response to surprise is in marked contrast to normal healthy functioning. The process of the healthy individual involves the continuous processing of data in order to physiologically decide whether to approach or avoid an object in the environment. However, when someone is surprised, the possibilities of responding, even on a

We Focus on Competency

Our goal is to have our students experience their competency again and again in all the work they do. This objective allows them to be more open to learning, and such openness leads them to increase their skills. As they become more competent, they begin to trust us more and to believe in their ongoing development and in themselves. When they leave our program, they feel confident to meet their work world in a new way, having first learned to believe in our competence and trust our feedback. And finally, they embrace their own competence.

We End Well

We teach that in a good ending people feel a completion and are ready to move on to the next experience. Incomplete endings sap energy, leaving the person stuck in the past and unable to move on to the next step. We work toward having our students leave excited about wanting to use all the things they have learned, and eager to put that new competency into action in their lives and work. We don't end anything quickly, and we leave time for a full ending whether it is during the first hour of our program or during a practicum. We pay attention to time limits and make

---

physiological level, are minimized. It is in that instant that the person is helpless, for he/she cannot approach or withdraw, open up or shut down. And it is at that instant in time, when resistances have been disarmed or circumvented, and one's normally smooth process has been disrupted, that one is most powerless and literally at the mercy of the other. Furthermore, it is at that instant, when one is startled and cannot resist, that one has no choice" (Melnick & S. Nevis, 1987, p. 47).

sure that students leave with a sense of achievement and completion and an ability to let go of our work so that they can move on to the next event in their lives.

In Closing

The creation of trust is essential for learning and growth to occur. Without trust why would any client listen to you? It starts with an expression of interest by the intervener that includes a mobilization of curiosity, attentiveness, and responsiveness. Trust building is two-way; it is an interactive process. Our first task is to create a trusting environment in which all are relaxed and open to impact. We do this by seeing and focusing on competence, and by using presence in a flexible way. We should point out that trusting is a dynamic process that at times waxes and wanes. In the course of our work, it increases and decreases. We are aware of when it is diminishing and call attention to its decrease.

12

INTERVENTION SKILLS

The Cape Cod Model is a high-impact approach. By this we mean that we do not just sit, observe, and nod our heads. We are "meddlers." We "meddle," not by offering advice, but by first *seeing* and noticing. Then we intervene in order to make a difference. How does this happen? We create and maintain trust throughout the entire process; it is an ongoing phenomenon, because without trust, positive change rarely occurs.

Next, we focus our attention on what is going on between individuals within the system, be it a dyad or a larger unit, and whether it takes place in therapy sessions, corporate meetings, or board retreats. Once we have gathered this knowledge, our task is to intervene by giving *feedback* and sharing our observations with clients. In most cases, when we tell people what we are noticing, if they are wise, they don't automatically accept it, even if there is established trust. There is almost always *resistance*, explicit or implicit. Resistance is a pull toward the status quo, to keeping the system dynamics, as problematic as they might be, the same. Resistance reflects an ambivalence toward change, because every system has positive characteristics, sometimes long-forgotten, that people want to preserve. Our way of noticing and managing resistance is one of the hallmarks of the Cape Cod Model; it continues throughout the intervention process.

Lastly, our model is unique because we believe that learning does not come simply from cognitive or emotional experiences. We assert that the locus of learning resides not only in the head but also in the body, and in the in-between of how people engage, relate, and interact with each other. We try something different so that the client can have a new experience. We call this dynamic *experiment*. We will describe these intervention skills in more detail below.

Seeing a System

Soft Eyes

Once enough trust has been generated so that we can all relax and our clients have given us permission to influence and teach them, we have to be able to view them with *soft eyes.* By so doing, we can see what is happening between them and the relational patterns as they emerge.

Joe: *I know that we have used the term* soft eyes *for years, but not soft ears, taste or other sensations. Do you remember how it originated?*

Sonia: *I actually have the memory of talking to a group about how we see and don't see. We talked about the difference between seeing and looking. In seeing, we are in a more relaxed state. We are waiting for something to come in, rather than searching for something, which is what we do when we are looking.*

Joe: *Yes. We are not asking for much with soft eyes. It is a much more receptive stance.*

Sonia: *Looking has a lot more energy.*

Joe: *I remember my first Gestalt training. We would take turns looking, closing our eyes, and looking some more. To look softly without any judgment or preconceptions was hard. To stay relaxed, to allow another to look*

190

into my eyes, was also difficult. I felt
tremendously vulnerable. No wonder they
call the eyes the pathway to the soul.

Sonia: *Yes, seeing with soft eyes is inviting the world
to come to you. Some parents or leaders wait
for their child to take things in at their own
pace, while others pull them into the world. It
is hard to strike the right balance.*

Joe: *Maybe the phrase* soft eyes *is misleading. It
could be replaced with relaxed or low energy.*

Sonia: *Yes, when we are relaxed, we are not
mobilized. We are not quickly grabbing at
something or projecting our wants and needs
onto the world. We are letting the world come
to us.*

Joe: *It is not so easy to do. It involves a bracketing
off of much of what we have been taught to
look for and stepping out of our habitual
ongoing experience.*

Sonia: *It is a combination of scanning and not
knowing what is going to happen next. Even
in saying this, I feel the fear. It can be
terrifying to be open to experience.*

During much of life we don't experience ourselves
seeing (listening, smelling, tasting, feeling). This is
because we spend most of our time in an automatic
mode focused on our needs and wants, and moving
through our day. Only when something interrupts our
ongoing experience—like having our car skid on a
slippery stretch of road, feeling a funny lump under our
arm, or being offered a new job that we have always
wanted—does awareness enter into our lives. But even
then, we often return very quickly to the status quo. This
lack of *seeing* is also true in our relationships, both
personal and professional.

As interveners, we serve our clients best when we

can *see* their habits and patterns. We scan for *the primary patterns that focus on energy: its rise, fall, location, speed, rhythm, movement, etc.* We have to see with flexibility, i.e., what we term *soft eyes.* This stance allows us to experience differently, just as a first-class painter is able to see in a different way from the rest of us.

Our stance is relaxed. Rather than searching for something, we wait for a pattern to emerge, an energetic form that occurs over and over again. When we notice something two or three times, we know that we have spotted one. When our clients are aware of their patterns, then choice and change become possible.

> **Joe:** *A few years ago, I went on safari in South Africa. We sat in open three-tiered vehicles with a tracker—the person who examined the terrain to determine where the animals were likely to be—sitting at the highest level. The rest of us also tried to see those tracks. Periodically, he would call out a signal to the driver to start heading in a direction that made no sense to the rest of us. More often than not, we would end up face to face with elephants, leopards, and rhinos. Despite my understanding that the tracker was searching for patterns, for different figure/ground relationships, I could never determine how he did it. I never got around to asking him if he could teach me to see animal prints. My hope is that if I had, he would have started with the basic patterns, and as I progressed, would have kept adding more complicated ones.*

There are a number of factors that keep us from *seeing patterns* between people. *First,* and one of the

192

most obvious, is that we are trained to notice patterns *within* individuals. This is particularly true for psychotherapists and coaches. It is quite different seeing what is happening between two or more people than within one. In fact, to do this requires a paradigm shift. *Second*, we are taught to look for causes. "When he does this, she does that." "When she does that, he does this." To be able to see the *co-creation* of an experience that all are doing together is a skill and an art. *Third*, we are taught to pay more attention to content and not process. Even when we are attuned to process, the mention of a topic, like a favorite song, can instantly pull us away from seeing and hearing.

Psychotherapists have created the terms *transference* and *countertransference* (Melnick, 2003) to describe major distractions from seeing and hearing clearly. These terms originally referred to incomplete and unaware remnants of a person's past that had tremendous impact on the present, influencing and often distorting the current experience. This *distortion of experience* not only occurs with individuals but also with couples, families, teams, and organizations. It is important to know that these distortions and distractions are normal and ongoing. They become problematic when we are unaware of them. This sort of *unfinished business* (see Table 2) not only keeps interveners from seeing with soft eyes and focusing on the process, but also contributes to our clients' inability to be present in the moment. We teach our students to know when this process is occurring. Usually becoming aware is enough for them to return to the present and assume a relaxed stance in which they can see again.

> **Joe:** *I was recently teaching in a country where laws about smoking in private are less stringent than in the USA and, even when they exist, they are not followed. I have had relatives die from*

193

smoking and have been involved with smoking cessation research. I had difficulty focusing on what was happening with the work team. I kept wanting to tell them to stop smoking. Rather than focusing on what was happening between them, I was being seduced by something in my past.

Two Ways of Seeing

For a number of years, we had not been satisfied with our students' ability to see an emerging pattern. We understood that as a faculty, we were skilled because of our training and our inherent ways of organizing. We all knew how to wait for patterns to emerge and to feel comfortable with disorganization, much like the American television detective Columbo (E. Nevis, 1987). Columbo seemed to have little direction as he investigated a crime. As he spoke to people his questions would wander, and so seemingly would his interest, as he waited for a pattern to emerge. This approach involved experiencing widely and loosely.

As we began working more with organizational consultants and leaders, people who lived in a more *strategic* world, we noticed that many of them organized very differently. They experienced in a more top down way, more by fitting experience into patterns, rather than waiting for patterns to emerge. This was much like the more focused approach of Sherlock Holmes. We quickly realized that you can notice and respond to patterns with both approaches. For our "Sherlock Holmes students," we created charts like the one below to support their way of learning to see patterns.

Table 7

SEEING PATTERNS
OF INTERACTION IN SYSTEMS

Sources of Patterns
- How energy is manifested: flow, type, level, direction, speed, movement, location, etc.
- How information/ideas are shared.
- How interest in one another is shown.
- How humor is used and shared.
- How rhythm and style appear.
- How they are able to be disappointed and/or disappoint.

Common Patterns That One Might See/Experience (Can be described as polarities)
- I *versus* We
- Being influenced *versus* being influential
- Giving each other space *versus* crossing the boundary in order to impact each other.
- Energy fixed in one place *versus* energy constantly shifting.
- Strategic interactions *versus* intimate interactions
- Focusing on one topic *versus* moving quickly across topics.
- More interested in focusing on sameness *versus* more interested in focusing on differences.
- Asking questions *versus* making statements.

"Boid" Rules and Seeing Emerging Patterns

We also supported our "Sherlocks" with a set of principles for organizing based on the "Boid" Rules developed in 1986 by Craig Reynolds. Boid, an artificial life software program replicates the act of bird flocking. The word *boid* is an abridged form of the term *bird-oid object*. Usually the complexity of interactions adheres to a set of simple rules. In the case of birds flocking, the rules are:

- Separation: Steer to avoid crowding flock mates.
- Alignment: Steer toward the average heading of flock mates.
- Cohesion: Steer to move toward the center of mass of the flock mates.

We have applied Boid to our teaching as a guide to help students notice emergent patterns in meetings.[32]

---

[32] Over the years, we have created Boid-like rules as a beginning structure for our Board meetings at GISC. We post them on a flip chart at each meeting along with our core values and some suggestions for how to have a good process.
- Address the hierarchy: recognize and make explicit the intimate versus strategic, the collaborative versus the hierarchical.
- Honor, respect, and appreciate the person behind the role.
- Create a safe space for people to speak.
- Create, maintain, and show curiosity and interest in people, differences, and tasks.
- Listen and make eye contact.
- Have a non-judgmental attitude.
- Focus on what is right, possible, and good, and remember that everyone is doing the best he or she can.
- Explore polarities fearlessly, and stay connected as we explore.

These adapted rules are:
- Each member of the group takes the appropriate share of space and time.
- People look at one another and address each other by name.
- People periodically sit back and scan the group to see what is going on.
- People ask each other questions, not only for information, but out of interest.
- People respond directly to questions.
- People allow themselves to influence and be influenced.

Some Final Thoughts on Seeing a Pattern

To *see* a system, one must be able to notice interactive patterns between the participants. It involves receptivity to perceiving these emerging figures. Learning to experience the materialization of phenomena, i.e., the coming together of disorganized pieces into a whole, has been the goal of our teaching about patterns for

---

- Give positive feedback.
- Be aware of the available time and help summarize and end.
- Laugh and have fun.

At our meetings we strive to create a healthy relational process to support the strategic work. For example, we rotate the role of "process observer" to two-person teams throughout the meetings. We work in modules with beginnings, middles, and ends in which we assess the just completed module both in terms of content and process. We also allow opportunities for people to participate in non-verbal ways. For example, there is a bowl of flowers that anyone can pick up if they want to say something but are having trouble getting in, and a bowl filled with small chocolates that board members can give to each other if they like what they are saying.

many years. But we were often unsuccessful in teaching our students to see in this way. Some began by favoring a more "Sherlock Holmes" method, one that involves fitting experience into patterns. Eventually, they experimented with developing the Colombo way of seeing and, in fact, many learned to be ambidextrous, using both approaches.

Feedback Focused

An effective intervention process is not one way, just from intervener to clients. Instead, it involves a process of continuous, mutual feedback. We pay particular attention to the giving and receiving of this—supportive—feedback that enhances learning and development. This is our primary form of teaching. We want our students to be immersed in feedback that interests and excites them. We want them to wake up every morning thinking about all they learned the day before, and excited about what the new day will bring. And, as in life, if yesterday was a tough day, they learn how to address *their* problem together. They learn that all challenges have a relational component. Living in a community that is relationally focused goes a long way in supporting people as they learn.

We understand that feedback can only be effective if we are open to it, and if it is presented in such a way that *sticks*, i.e., has long-term influence on our lives and who we are. In order to be integrated, it needs to be more than immediately impactful. It needs to be memorable.[33] Negative feedback seems to be accepted

---

[33] Chip and Dan Heath (2007) describe how to craft a "sticky" message. They outline characteristics of ideas that create "stickiness," such as simplicity, addressing a gap in our knowledge, emotional appeal, and creating a believable story. The therapist, coach, consultant, or leader makes the feedback stick through a set of skills.

very easily, remaining in our body much longer than the positive (Damasio, 1994). It decreases our openness to taking in new experiences and making sense of the world. It *diminishes possibilities.*

For most of us, positive feedback has less inherent stickiness, and this is certainly understandable. But is it true? Who hasn't been misled or seduced by flattery? Who hasn't been let down by a trusted friend? Who hasn't felt the embarrassment of letting one's guard down upon hearing the *positive*, only to have it followed by *the real message,* a negative one? Many of us grew up with a parent saying, "You did a nice job on this, but . . ." Kids are smart. They quickly learn to be suspicious of the first positive part, while bracing for the negative. Sadly, a version of this is even taught in organizational training as a *feedback sandwich*—something negative enclosed between two slices of positive. Our primary focus is to teach our students to see competency and to give feedback based on what they see and hear; feedback that is authentic and opens everyone up to learning (Melnick and S. Nevis, 2005).

Feedback Skills

We have all received feedback that not only has helped us grow and develop but also that has been ineffective, and even damaging. Figuring out what to say to someone, how to create a climate so that the person wants to hear it, and how to say it so it takes hold requires skill. Our first task is setting up the conditions in which feedback is sought and desired. We do this in many ways. As said previously, we constantly invite questions, balance our interventions, avoid surprises, etc.

The type of feedback we teach our students to give

---

is largely about patterns. There is much to notice about people engaging with each other. It takes discipline to hold back and not grab the first thing we see, but instead to wait for a pattern to emerge. We often tell our students only to give feedback about patterns that they have seen at least three times. Of course, there has much written on the concept of feedback (e.g., D. Bohm and L. Nichol, 2004; W. Isaacs, 1999; M. Rosenberg, 2012; D. Stone and S. Heen, 2015; D. Stone and B. Patton, 2010; D. Yankelovich, 2001). We summarize some of our thoughts below (see Table 8).

Table 8

SALIENT POINTS ABOUT FEEDBACK

- Feedback is always experience based. It rests on what we see and hear.
- We pay attention to which feedback is useful. We notice how the feedback is received and its impact. Is it taken in and swallowed too easily, or pushed away with a deflective comment?
- Feedback is always relational and ongoing. There is always *feedback about our feedback.*
- When we tell people something about themselves, they always respond, even if the response is non-verbal. It is important to notice this and ask about it.
- Feedback, in its essence, is often an addition to awareness or a correction. You are telling someone something about themselves that they might not know. Even when positive, it is often hard to accept and is often difficult to swallow. This can be embarrassing.
- We use interpretations sparsely, especially ones where we guess how the past impacted the present.

Feedback as Caricaturing

Caricatures are hard to change because most of us gravitate toward people (as well as newspapers, television shows, churches) that share our views; we often look for experiences to support those views and ignore ones that challenge them. No wonder patterns are so hard to change. Caricaturing is not all bad, and, in fact, is essential for helping to bring order to a basically chaotic world. It would be scary to think what life would be like if we had to pay attention to everything. Also, caricatures are sometimes correct, or at least contain a grain of truth.

When we label others, we lose the ability to see the growth steps that are actually occurring. When we label someone as generous, spacey, aggressive, etc., we may fail to see them when they are stingy, focused, and passive. If we mark them as obsessive, histrionic, narcissistic, or a projector, we stop paying attention to everything else that they are. We stop noticing that we are projecting onto someone(s) who are also part of what is happening (between us), even if the other is not physically present (Melnick and S. Nevis, 1997).

We never tell people who they are, but instead what they *do*. If we tell them that they are wonderful and the feedback is not connected to what they did, it will stir up complicated feelings. This occurs not just in the person receiving the feedback, but in everyone else present, as everyone tries to figure out what we mean.

We work hard not to compare people or place them in hierarchies and categories, especially the *easy ones,* like thinkers/feelers, introverted/extroverted, and strategic/relational. When such comparisons or categorizations happen, potential is lost and many people are unhappy. The above is also true in terms of the systems with which we work. Even if we use positive labels such as creative, involved, hardworking, etc., we understand that we are running the risk of generating a caricature, of *always* seeing people in this way and, as a result, not noticing when they are not creative, uninvolved, and relaxed.

Some Final Thoughts on Caricaturing

As relational beings, we are always involved in a continuous feedback process with others. We teach our students to see and then give feedback about recurring patterns that fall outside the awareness of the individual(s). When the feedback is presented in a way that *sticks,* then new possibilities appear. We present feedback in a balanced way, seldom singling out an individual, and always inviting dialogue about the feedback, so that it can become meaningful. (Of course, the singling out of individuals is more acceptable when there is a positional leader and a fixed hierarchy.) When feedback is considered, changes can emerge.

Our interventions at the beginning usually involve feedback designed to increase awareness. We start by asking such questions as, "Have the (two of you, the team, family, workgroup, etc.) noticed . . ." And it is almost always about what is well developed; a pattern that is noticed and identified as a competence.

If our presence is accepted, and a minimal degree of trust has been created, we usually don't experience much resistance at this point. But if we do notice it, we engage it. Later, when we illuminate the cost or the

202

price our clients pay for an overdeveloped competence, this feedback often generates more resistance. How we identity and address this resistance is described in detail below.

Resisting and Resistances

Joe: *One of the Gestalt values I find most helpful is our belief in the usefulness of moving toward differences.*

Sonia: *That's what a good conversation is because everyone knows pieces of things and everybody's wants are different. Differences create energy.*

Joe: *And we also understand that we are naturally wary of differences. The biologically ingrained suspicion of difference is often the stimulus for much of the suffering in our intimate relationships and the world.*

Sonia: *Yet, if not for differences, life would be boring. I focus on differences a lot when I'm teaching. When people resist them, we teach our students to move toward the resistant people. It changes things. Once a good conversation gets going, people who don't like to talk find themselves talking. And we welcome their criticism as well as their praise. There's always a piece of truth in every criticism. This is because we see one thing and they another. We can't say we are accurate, and they are not. We can't know everything. So, we are open to learning from them. We are learning together. We teach them, and they teach us. It's what keeps the world moving. It's about being open to another's experience. The world is wide.*

Joe: *Whenever there are forces for change, it will* *generate the opposite forces for sameness. This is not only true between individuals, or within groups and organizations, but also, internally. It seems that there is always resistance. And If I am not getting any overt resistance, it doesn't mean that it is not there. It probably means it is underground* (Perls, 1969).

Sonia: *When we teach the Cape Cod Model, we emphasize the positives in the beginning. But after a while, the negative begins to emerge strongly, and we welcome it. Both sides are necessary. We always need many sides, and if we call the other side resistant, then we won't be open to it.*

Joe: *I remember in my original Gestalt training program, we were asked to scan the group and pick a quality that someone had and we didn't like. We then had to go up to that person and say, "I am a secret admirer of your (fill in the blank—coldness, passivity, charm, etc.). Would you be willing to tell me how this quality benefits you?" And I still remember a person in that program I couldn't stand. I thought he was stupid, sloppy, and sentimental. The group leader led me to understand that these were disowned parts of myself, and my work was to become friendlier with these parts by becoming friends with this individual. I also began to see the value of behaviors that I had previously characterized negatively.*

Resistance and Righteousness

Joe: *This talk about owning disowned parts of myself reminds me of the concept of* *righteousness. We work hard not to be righteous; we don't judge people in our model. That's why our Center has developed a reputation for welcoming other programs' "failures" into our programs.*

Sonia: *When we find ourselves resisting others, we take a look at what we're resisting. As you realized, it's often a disowned part of ourselves. Many in the world are interested in people who think the same way as they do and confirm their worldviews. They think they know what's right. No one knows what's right. It simply can't be. While we are saying to move towards differences, the world and our country are telling us to move towards similarities.*

Joe: *When each one knows what is right, nothing happens. But it's not only that nothing happens, people are hurt by this stance.*

Sonia: *So how do we teach people to be less righteous?*

Joe: *I know that in our programs we have always looked for diversity, and we stand up for that. We work hard at bringing diverse people together, and we teach them how to be interested. And if they can't be, then we look at their resistance to being interested.*

Sonia: *The world is moving more and more into a type of psychological polarization.*

Joe: *Yes, and it is too bad. Many of us seem to associate with people who think the way we do—politically, religiously, financially, psychologically, etc. We tend to read papers and watch television shows that confirm our beliefs; and when we come up against contradictory information, we learn to dismiss it.*

Joe recalls a conversation he had with someone espousing an opposing point of view.

> I had just landed, exhausted from an overnight international flight. I boarded a shuttle van to my hotel and found myself sitting next to a well-dressed American deep in conversation with a European couple seated behind him. My semi-dreamlike state was punctured by a series of phrases from this man. "Obama is a lot like Hitler. He also took power during a time of economic depression. Do you know that children in America are taught to say, 'Hail Obama'? He really is a foreigner; he was not born in the United States."
>
> I felt rage—and, yes, contempt began quickly to build inside me. I struggled whether to speak or to remain silent; knowing that speaking from my anger might feel good in the moment but ultimately would serve no purpose. I also knew that I could not remain silent. Taking a breath, I tapped him on the knee, smiled, and said, "I want you to know that I disagree with basically everything you have been saying since I entered this van." He looked startled and surprised. I then said, "I rarely have an opportunity to discuss things with people who have your political beliefs. My guess is that this is the same for you." He nodded slowly and began to relax.
>
> I then said, "It is too bad that people who feel so passionately about our country as the two of us rarely get an opportunity to have a good conversation." He relaxed further, and slowly we began to talk. To be truthful, he was mainly doing the talking and I the listening. But in my listening, I continually reminded him in a soft

206

way that I disagreed with him nearly 100%, but I also told him that I was interested in his thoughts because, as I put it, "I rarely get to hear people with your views." As I was leaving the van, he held out his hand and said that it was too bad we were staying at different hotels, because he would have liked to have had a drink with me and talk further. I told him that I agreed with him.

Did I change any of his views? I doubt it. But I do hope I created a little bit of openness on his part with respect to other perspectives. As for me, I do know that I was able to speak up and move on (Melnick and S. Nevis, 2010, p. 229).

What Are Resistances?

All the early psychoanalytically-oriented theories believed that therapy was designed to help people give up resisting and accept what life dealt them. Much of therapeutic work was spent looking at how patients were resisting; not only in accepting their past, but also with respect to the therapy and the therapist.

Traditional psychoanalytic theory postulated the concepts of *defenses* (such as introjection and projection) as ways of warding off anxiety—an unavoidable byproduct of living in this world. The early Gestalt theorists believed differently. They believed that these defenses—renamed resistances, were *overdeveloped patterns of people doing the best they could.* This is true whether for an individual, couple, family, group, team, or organization.

While still emphasizing the negative of these *common fixed patterns or habits,* these early Gestaltists also saw that they helped us creatively adjust to life's twists and turns (E. Polster and M. Polster, 1973). They understood that all resistances can be both positive and negative. Let us give you one example. The resistance

207

of *retroflection* is a physical turning inward. It is doing to and for myself what I wish to do to others, or have others do to or for me. It is an efficient way to soothe myself when no one else is available. Biting my tongue is useful, when speaking my anger out loud could get me punished. However, retroflecting also cuts me off from others. So, to hug myself when others are open to hugging me, or to bite my tongue when others are open to hearing my annoyance, diminishes possibilities for growth and relationship.[34]

Originally, all the *resistances* were used conceptually by therapists working with individual cleints, referring only to what the client was doing, not to the relational context (Merry and Brown, 1987). Unfortunately, resistances were often taught as characerological aspects of individuals so that, for example, people would be labeled as *deflectors* or *projectors*. This way of viewing resistances is contrary to our beliefs. Labeling people locks us into a reified past and stands in the way of seeing possibilities. Although informed by our past memories, and by our hopes and dreams for the future, all we have is the present.

Sonia: *A number of years ago, I was teaching a module on resistance. I began to notice that there was something wrong with viewing resistance patterns as belonging only to the individual, instead of to relationships. This perspective has become basic to the Cape Cod Model; we are all responsible for what happens between us. When something happens between two or more people, all are*

---

[34] The other common resistances, beside *projection* and *introjection,* include *confluence, desensitization, deflection,* and *egotism* (see M. Polster and E. Polster, 1973).

contributing. *There is no such thing as a bystander.*[35]

Joe: *Here is another example. I might project (guess) that you love me, hate me, etc., but you have a role in either allowing this projection to stand or in challenging it. This understanding that resistances and resisting are always relational has helped us look at what is happening in the "in between," and moved us away from viewing individuals as separate from each other and their environment (Wollants, 2012). This perspective allows us to view situations as always fluid and dependent on two or more persons for their creation.*

As change agents, we often work with clients who are *resistant* to trying new things. They continuously focus on the negative. In our everyday world, most of us avoid these judgmental people because being with them dispirits us. However, we often end up working with them as clients. We understand that people who avoid seeing the good in things are protecting themselves from re-experiencing the pain they felt in their lives when their hopes were shattered. But the cost of this stance is immense, for they also give up the possibility of feeling really good.

Joe: *In the Cape Cod Model, when working with such clients, we do not meet their negativity with criticism or avoidance. We don't join them in their despair; but we do join them.*

---

[35] We are all aware that trauma can occur when we are watching an upsetting event, even if not directly involved; like watching someone bully another (see Mortola, Hiton, and Grant, 2007).

	We *"hold their hands" until they are able to bear the pain of losing. And losing is painful.*
Sonia:	*Nor are we interested in changing them. Their negativity does not push us away. We accept them as they are. Because we become interested in them, they are apt to get interested in us.*
Joe:	*We do not wish to change or resist who they are, or what they think, feel, believe, and say. We do not have a wish for them to be different. Because of this stance, mutual trust begins to develop, and we can become a team that works together. Trust does not happen instantly. It takes time.*
Sonia:	*The first Gestalt concept I fell in love with was the importance of resisting as necessary for living. When I had my babies, they all learned to say no before yes. No before yes seems to be part of our biological wiring. From the start, resisting is a necessary part of life.*

Being Able to Say No

The ability to resist is as necessary as the ability to go along—not to resist. We tend to undervalue *no* in our development, not appreciating the fact that a *no* lays the groundwork for being able to go forward in the world. To say it simply, *if you can't say no, you can't say yes.* The belief that *no* is a bad word is ingrained for many in our society. We are taught to be nice and polite; to say thank you for a present even if we don't like it. This overvaluing of yes and devaluing of no is often found in our institutions and organizations as well. It results in large losses because it diminishes creativity and results in burnout. One result of our *yes culture* is that people don't know how to say or hear a no. We can learn to say no as respectfully as yes. Rather than seeing the word no as aggressive and a hindrance to dialogue, it can instead be viewed as a builder of trust and essential for intimacy.

Joe: *A former client of mine called me in a mess. It seemed that he had gotten himself involved with four women, two seriously. A man usually of high moral values, he was puzzled and appalled as to how he could have done such a thing. As we talked, it became clear that he could not tolerate saying no—to hearing the sound of the word, to feeling the sensations, or to seeing the impact on others.*

We briefly probed his childhood. A therapist himself, he had received much therapy in the past and knew many of the reasons for his behavior; but this knowledge wasn't helping him much. We created a plan to help him with his dilemma. He understood that for nearly all of us, our first impulse is to say yes, especially to people we care about. However, in our complicated world, there is a cost to the quick yes. His assignments were as follows.

First, when dealing with a request, he had to say, "I need to think about it and will get back to you," and keep the promise. He found that, in time, his initial response to say yes often turned to no.

Then he agreed to say no three times a day. As he struggled with this assignment, he decided that he would think of each no as the equivalent of a good workout at a gym. (He hated to exercise but did it religiously for his long-term health. He always felt good after a workout.) He came in the next week proud of himself, saying that he was able to say no three times a day and, to his surprise, people seemed to accept no easily.

Next, we talked about the easy no and the hard no, the ones that few of us like to hear or say, the ones that result in hurt or angry feelings. This task would be the most difficult. He was to say a hard no twice when a big part of him wanted to say yes, but a bigger part wanted to say no. He learned how to say no with regret.

Finally, he had to approach the person to whom he had said a hard no, ask him or her how s/he felt having heard it, and continue the conversation. He struggled to bear his sensations and reactions to the person's response and to talk it through.

Ultimately, he was able respectfully to end the two peripheral relationships and is struggling to summon up the courage to be more authentic with each of the two women about whom he cares more deeply. He talks about himself as a work-in-progress.

Some Final Thoughts on Resisting and Resistances

We understand that what we call *resisting* often happens when people are experiencing different realities. We are usually called in because people (couples, families, work teams, organizations) are not happy with the way things are. As interveners, we understand that the more we advocate for, or are seen as supporters of, change, the more the forces for the status quo, for keeping things the way they are, will get mobilized. The issue is not whether resistance is generated. It always is because people's values, experience, and behavior are often different. The art of a change professional is to allow resistances to surface, and to respect their legitimacy, i.e., not to shame the *resisters*, but to invite them into dialogue, to lean into the resistance, and to join them. It is this joining that helps create a unique trusting relationship.

When our clients discover that they are able to disagree openly, object and push back, and that this opposition is actually welcomed and encouraged, then the ground for a unique trusting relationship has been laid. Most important is to remember that resistance is simply a different perspective, and a normal part of relationships between people.

As interveners, we become interested in resistance. We move towards it. We give resistance legitimacy by embracing and welcoming it. A clear yes and a clear no are wonderful, but sometimes the responses called for are more complex and nuanced. We teach our students to respond authentically and clearly.

> **Joe:** *A colleague of mine recently told me of an experience she had in a therapy supervision group. Out of the blue, a supervisee said to the supervisor, "Would you sleep with me?" Shocked at what he had said, he turned red and started to apologize to her. Rather than resisting or mobilizing quickly, she sat back and said, "Please let me think about it." After a minute or two, she looked him in the eye and said, stretching her hands about a foot apart, "This part of me would like to sleep with you." Then, stretching her hands a foot and a half apart, she added, "This much of me would not."*

Experiment

The Cape Cod Model is grounded in an *experimental attitude* that has been a cornerstone of the Gestalt approach since its beginning. This attitude involves a willingness to experiment with behaviors without a preset assumption of what should or will happen. Exploring patterns with awareness and support is what Gestaltists call a *safe emergency* (Perls et al., 1951). It is an emergency in that it is action-oriented and just difficult enough to arouse anxiety, and it is safe in that there is adequate support present. By support, we mean a non-authoritarian and non-corrective respect for the clients' experience (Wheeler and Axellson, 2015). To repeat, our optimistic orientation leads to a belief that we can learn and grow from any situation by acting, behaving, and moving, if there is appropriate awareness and adequate support.

This is because the supportive *presence* of an intervener and a focus on becoming aware of entrenched patterns is often enough for change to occur. The creation of a supportive *dialogue* (contact) in which the client's thoughts and feelings are explored within a frame of *well-developed versus less developed, developing,* or *next developmental step* is also often enough to impact highly resistant patterns. But frequently something else may be needed to untangle and loosen these patterns. It is at this point that the intervener might suggest an experiment, a form of doing, a "Try this" (Melnick, 1980).

Experiment Versus Technique

The Gestalt approach emerged in the 1960s as one of the most popular of the humanistic psychotherapies. It became popular, in part, because it added an experimental dimension (a task, a doing) that was absent in the dialogical formats that formed the cornerstone of most of the humanistic approaches. Fritz Perls was a master at creating experiments in the moment to increase awareness, explore polarities, and sometimes to simply try something different. However, what started out as Perls's creative process soon became popularized and turned into specific exercises and techniques designed with specific goals in mind. Unlike experiments, exercises and techniques are often prepared in advance to direct clients toward a specific objective or piece of learning. The intervener actively structures the session by offering the clients particular tasks.

Joe: *I remember being taught to place a person with whom we have unfinished business in an empty chair and speak to them, with the goal being the completion of unfinished business.*

Sonia: *Yes, another common one was having a two-chair dialogue between a set of polarities, often parts of ourselves, like our playful and serious sides.*

Joe: *We were taught to not look at one side or the other but to look for the relational pattern, much like we teach out students today. But we are not looking for the relationship with internal parts of our clients but between them, others and the system as a whole.*

Sonia: *Yes, and the biggest distinction between experiments and exercises is whether the goal is to teach a specific piece of content (exercise) or whether the intent is to explore. Exploring involves embracing an attitude of "What would happen if?"* (Melnick, 1980; Roubal, 2009). *Both exercises and experiments are useful; we just need to be clear as to which we are using.*

Joe: *I remember taking graduate courses in workshop and laboratory design, in which the distinction was very clear. We were taught to create exercises to facilitate specific learning. The organizational development market place is filled with many handbooks that detail exercises for any situation* (Pfeiffer and Jones, 1975; Holman and Devane, eds., 1999).

Sonia: *Yes. When I'm teaching team-building I might begin by asking all members of the group to* *select another, whom they experience as being very different from them, to address them directly and begin a two-minute conversation in front of the rest of the team. Sometimes I have a specific goal in mind. Sometimes I am just curious.*

Creating Experiments

The Gestalt approach primarily focuses on the here and now. Much of its original popularity was based on having clients expand their awareness of what they were doing in the present. We both recall many training programs in which hours were spent becoming aware of the sensations of touching, tasting, hearing, and seeing; of exploring emotions such as hurt, anger, sadness, and joy; and of giving and receiving feedback about how we impact others. In our Cape Cod Model, we still emphasize increasing awareness, but rather than being individually and internally focused, we ask our clients to notice the *in between*, i.e., what *they* are doing together.

Although there is almost always *resistance* generated when anything new and different is introduced in a session, it tends to increase when people become aware of the cost of their relational patterns, and even more so when we suggest trying something new in the moment. Unfortunately, awareness is sometimes not enough to generate change. We sometimes have to act and practice, so that new concepts and learning get into our bones. We all remember studying for examinations and having the learning fade quickly as soon as we put down our pens. Experiments allow us to ground the new learning in our bodies.

The implementation of experiment is dependent on first creating a trusting intervener/client relationship.

216

Experiments usually begin with a suggestion from the intervener to try something different *based on previous work.* They are often a continuation of a theme that is brought into the here and now. Although experiments can be created at any time during an interaction, the more complex ones usually occur during the latter parts of sessions.

The intervener's first task is to spark the clients' interest and curiosity, usually by giving a rationale for trying something different and by getting an agreement to move forward. It is also important that the experiment is co-created; that both clients and interveners have a role in shaping it. Once begun, the intervener's task is to pay attention to *fit,* noticing whether it is too difficult or too easy. At any point, the intervener can interrupt to check out how it is going and to alter it, often making it either easier or harder. We call this concept *grading* (Zinker, 1978). The experiment is followed by a *debrief* in which the experience is *fattened,* by discussing what was learned (Roubal, 2009).

As mentioned above, many of the original experiments focused on increasing internal awareness of feelings or embodied patterns, but others involved exploring connections between polarities or splits in the individual, such as top dog/underdog, input versus output, I versus we, low energy versus high energy, or shoulds versus wants. In the Cape Cod Model, our experiments tend to be relational in nature, include everyone, and focus on what is less developed or developing before our eyes. For example, in a system that is high energy and output oriented, the intervener might notice that people speak quickly with a sense of urgency, rarely addressing each other directly. After discussing the positives and then the costs of this way of being together, the intervener might suggest an experiment. "Would everyone agree to take one breath before speaking, or to speak to only one individual by looking at them and addressing them by name? Or . . .

Joe: *I remember conducting a retreat with the leadership team of a large state agency. The leader was very relational and supportive of the team. Prior to the meeting, I met with each of the team. They all felt very connected and expressed concerns as to how they would manage with the upcoming staff cuts that had been hinted from above. They respected their immediate leader but were concerned as to how hard she had been working to keep the team together. They feared she was becoming burnt out.*

As they began their conversation, I noticed that all group members would direct their comments to the leader, and she would always respond fully. When one team member would occasionally address a colleague, the leader would intervene and insert herself into the conversation. No one on the team objected. As a result, most of the group energy was usually focused on the leader. I first pointed out the positives of this pattern; how engaged the leader was in the task and how welcoming the team was with her involvement. After a while, I moved to the cost of those patterns and what was underdeveloped. The leader was becoming exhausted, and the creation of dyads and work groups to address issues rarely happened.

The team agreed to try an experiment in which the leader sat back and the team members worked with each other, only bringing in the leader when they had a question or were stuck. As the experiment progressed, the leader relaxed in her chair and the team members began to build on each other's ideas. Because they did it so easily I suggested as part of the debrief, that the leader tell the team what they did well, and that the team describe how it was to

218

experience the leader in a different mode.

Some Final Thoughts on Experiments

Our purpose in experimenting is either to explore redundant relational patterns, or to try out new ways of interacting. In the Cape Cod Model, experiment typically comes after the client system has become aware of patterns that may no longer be useful in the current situation, and of the price that people pay for constantly returning to them. We then invite their curiosity about both the usefulness and limitations of these patterns. We suggest an experiment by clearly articulating simple instructions that are balanced and address all members of the system. We look for resistance and *lean into it.* We engage the system in trying it and coach them through it, paying attention as to whether it is too simple or too hard (grading). We then debrief it, asking what it was like for them and what they learned.

SECTION FOUR

PUTTING IT ALL TOGETHER

13

THE CAPE COD TRAINING PROGRAM

As we approach the end of this book, we would like to describe our training model in detail, integrating many of the concepts outlined previously. We hope it will make sense, both in terms of its concepts and as a potent way to help people grow and develop.

As we teach the model, we break it down into a step-by-step progression that mirrors the Cycle of Experience. We strive for a good beginning by first creating trust, always working to increase it, and noticing when it is stagnant or diminishing. This mutual trust allows us to create a hierarchy in which the individuals and group will work with us. We teach following the principles outlined earlier. We establish a learning community in which both mistakes and successes are applauded, and learning is continuous. We create an ending in which the participants are able to talk about what they have learned. As they describe their learning, it begins to become more integrated, more a part of them. Then energy subsides and they are able to move on to their next experience.

The model as practiced is always sensitive and responsive to changing contexts. As we said in the beginning, Gestalt, like jazz, is improvisational, and the working situation is always changing. Nonetheless, if you were to look at a session of any of the faculty teaching and supervising, it would be easy to understand what we are doing.

Our Training Model

Overall Design

What follows is a description of our core training program: the sixteen-day, two session introduction to the *Cape Cod Model.* We want to show you what we teach, how we teach it, and how the two are connected to our organizing beliefs and principles. Our program is *practice heavy,* for the best way to learn is by *doing.* It is by doing that the theory becomes a part of us. Therefore, our participants spend a large part of their time working in randomly assigned practicum groups of six. We try our best to keep these groups together throughout the entire sixteen days of our program.

During each eight-day session, each participant is paired with another to work as interveners. During week one, each pair also serves as a *client couple* for the other *interveners.* Two other individuals act as *observers.* We explain to each client couple that this is not a role play, and we ask them to be who they are, *real and authentic.* During the second week, the participants continue as intervening pairs, but they no longer serve as client couples. The client couples are disbanded so that the practicum groups can be reformed as either client families or client work teams for the intervening pairs. Participants are asked to make the roles real, and it is amazing how quickly this happens.

A Day in the Life of the
Cape Cod Model Training Program

Community Meetings

We start each morning with a community meeting that is led by one of us. The purpose is to bring us all together, to clear up any leftover confusion, to deal with unfinished business, and to describe the practicum task for the day. We often present a short lecture, the content of which focuses on a step-by-step development of the Cape Cod Model. The meeting is leader-focused, with the faculty member on display, rarely knowing what issue will be thrown his or her way. At these meetings questions are encouraged. As we go through the structure of the meeting, we all know that everyone in the room is paying attention to much more than the content of the conversation.

Lectures and Demonstrations

Both weeks are filled with lectures and experiential exercises designed to emphasize different parts of the model, such as *how to see a system, the impact of unfinished business, presence, working with resistance,* etc. Each lecture contains an important experiential component and has a length of no more than one hour. Faculty always demonstrate the model using real invited couples, families, work teams, and organizations.

We put ourselves in such a vulnerable position for a number of reasons. We believe that good leaders and educators should not ask their followers to do what they are unwilling to do. It is a real-life example of leaders moving between strategy and intimacy, and it allows us to teach by having the students observe us in a more vulnerable context. It also lets them relax.

We bring in couples, families, teams, and organizations at the end of the program, because we want our trainees to see the faculty working with people whom we don't know, and who don't know anything about the model. We do this so that the students can begin to have confidence that the skills they are learning are useful not just in the program but also out in the real world. It is reassuring to the students that the model actually works *out there.*

We should reiterate here that we also offer an optional third week designed for participants with an organizational focus. They are given an opportunity to work in small groups with organizational teams that join us for a day of consultation, knowing little about our model.[36] We have just begun offering another additional week where we explore concepts such as resistance and experiment in greater detail.

Practicum: Engagement and Intervention

As discussed above in the sections on trust and presence, there is a skill in learning how to engage a couple, family, or business group. How do we connect with a family that has a mother, grandmother, baby, and an adolescent boy; or a leadership group consisting of a CEO, CFO, and two vice presidents who are the heirs apparent? Do we interact differently with a group of four than with a group of twelve? What if it is a short-term work group, or a three-generational family business? And whom do we speak to first? Do we start with the mother or the teen, with the CEO, or the junior V.P.? How do we connect with the leader in such a way that the group also feels seen and acknowledged? We spend a great deal of time teaching our students how to engage people. The following is what we tell them.

Instructions for Successful Engagement of Clients

(1) Describe to Your Clients What You're Going to Do

---

[36] For a fuller description of this module see: http://gisc.org/practitioners/programs/CapeCodTrainingPro gram-Practitioners-GestaltInternationalStudyCenter.php

Tell your clients about the structure of the session, and what will be asked of them. Encourage them to say if they are confused, and ask if they need or want more information. Tell them what is coming. This allows them to relax and be in the moment, rather than wondering what will happen next. Throughout the entire session, look for any confusion or resistance to what you are describing, and view these moments as opportunities to create trust.

(2) Ask Your Clients to Talk to Each Other

After connecting with your clients, ask them to talk to each other, explaining that you are going to pull back and observe. Tell them that you are interested in *how* they are with each other, and that the best way to see this is to watch them interact. Then ask them if this makes sense. At this point, people often experience some surprise or resistance to interacting in this way. They might say, "We talk to each other all the time." If they are bold, they might say, "We were expecting you to speak *to* us, to tell us what to do or how to solve our dilemma." Sometimes they will say nothing, but it will be obvious from their bodily responses that there is some resistance to following your instructions. This point is often critical in the development or diminishment of trust.

Rather than move on, we welcome their concerns and deal with them in a clear and respectful manner. This willingness to join clients when they express objections or criticisms is essential for establishing trust. During these times, all the clients—not just the one being critical—is paying attention to how you respond. If the *objector* is treated respectfully and sees that it is possible to challenge, be confused, ask for more, or deviate from your instructions, there emerges a type of openness that is necessary for good learning.

227

(3) Invite Your Clients to Feel Free to Turn to You

Tell them that you are going to sit back, but that they should feel free to turn to you at any time. We do this for at least two reasons. First, we don't want anybody to wonder what we are thinking. If they are curious, we want them to ask, and we want to respond in a full and contactful way. If they are wondering, but not asking, it breaks their connection with you and their family members, partners, and colleagues. Second, we believe in the importance of teaching people to turn to others when they feel stuck or confused. To stay too long in confusion is not useful. Our goal is to help create and maintain a conversation that flows, a conversation that allows everyone, clients and interveners, to talk to each other about important issues.

(4) Observe the Clients Interacting

Watching people interact is not easy. It requires an ability to *see widely* and to scan as we look for certain patterns. (Remember the tracker in the African safari referred to above?) We want you to focus on the interactions between people, waiting until some pattern emerges that will interest and engage your clients.

At this point, our students sometimes forget that our goal at this stage is to observe the interactional process happening in the here and now. The students often revert to their old habit of listening to the content, because content is more easily accessible intellectually and more understandable. It is also very seductive. It is natural for our students to be interested in the content. Our work is different. It is to get them interested in the process—into the *how,* not the *it* or the *why.*

Another common mistake our students make is to move into the role of *expert* and begin giving advice. It

228

is our experience that most people have considered much of the advice we can offer them. Often, giving unsolicited advice allows the student to feel more confident and less confused. Yet a willingness to stay with confusion is a core skill of our approach. And advice, especially advice that has *not* been solicited, often says more about the helper than the client system.

It also is a mistake to focus on the individual at the expense of the group, a point that we have discussed above. This kind of focusing pulls us away from what is happening in the *in between.* In large part, it has to do with the helper's unaware needs, biases, and unfinished business (see *Table 1,* "Signs of Unfinished Business).

In sum, by *observing* we mean that we look for a pattern or a process that our clients are using over and over again, and that we see as a demonstration of their competence. The pattern often (though not always) involves the ways in which energy is managed in the relationship. For example, we might notice that this twosome is filled with such *powerful interest* that they finish each other's sentences, leaning forward and matching each other blow for blow as they disagree. We notice the speed and the liveliness. We are not paying much attention to labeling them as arguing, for that is not a *description* of a process. We know that there is always a price to pay for any competency. But now is not the time to bring it up. It is too soon in your relationship with them. Besides, they might figure it out by themselves. Remember the paradoxical theory of change?

(5) Interrupt Your Clients

Remember when you told them you were going to pull back and watch them, and then tell them what you see? This is how you do it. Interrupt them by leaning in, and even moving your chair closer to them to stop them. Some people find it annoying, and others appreciate that you are going to tell them something you saw. First, talk to them about how they feel about being interrupted, and then tell them you will talk with your partner and then tell them what you noticed.

Many of our students have difficulty interrupting. Some avoid it for a host of reasons. Others interrupt like "bulls in a china shop." If the clients can't hear you, or are jarred by your interruptions, then they will have difficulty taking in what you say. There is an art to approaching clients slowly, so that they become interested in us, and in what we have to say, before we say it.

(6) Talk with Your Intervener-Partner

Pull back after inviting your clients to listen as you talk with your colleague about them, and pay attention to whether they are listening. We see this talking not only as an opportunity to share what the two of you have noticed and figure out how to say it, but also to have them see how the two of you talk to each other. Remember that this discussion is also an intervention, which is different from when you are addressing them face-to-face. Because you are not speaking directly to them, we find that they are often more open to what you are saying, and resistance is minimized.

As you talk with your partner, you are jointly shaping the intervention and your clients may see you agreeing quickly or even disagreeing. Talk for just enough time so that you are clear as to what you want to say to them. This *talking to each other* allows the clients to get a glimmer of what you are noticing, and what you will tell them. Thus, by the time you turn to them, they are somewhat prepared as to what they are going to hear. Remember, one of our goals is to minimize surprise. (Sometimes when we are working alone we will ask our clients if they mind if we say our thoughts out loud so that we can figure out what we wish to say to them. This also allows our clients to be prepared for what we might tell them.)

(7) Find a Pattern That Interests you

Look for patterns in your clients' process, not in their content, ones that are connected to what you are seeing and hearing in the moment. Then you need to figure out how to say it in a way that interests them; a way that they will understand and care about. If a client is confused about what you are seeing or challenges you, you need data to back it up. Having the data available is not as hard as it sounds, because we only see things that interest us, and interesting things are easier to grasp.

Here is an instance about how we have been developing the model. For many years, we would ask our students to stop the clients when they saw a competency, and turn to them to present what they saw, along with the supporting data. But we found that sharing this data without it being asked for often confused people. So, for example, we might come to a conclusion that a group is passionate, and we want them to know it because it is a good thing. Back then, we used to give them the following data: "You talk with loud voices, have good eye contact, and lean in as you speak." Now we simply give them the observation. If they accept what we have said, we do not say more. But if they ask what we mean when we say *passionate,* then we give them the data. Too much unasked-for information diminishes stickiness (Heath and Heath, 2007).

It is still important to hold the information that led to what we tell our clients, even if they never ask. This is necessary because, in working with clients, we are constantly gathering information, and more data gets added as the work continues. There are often opportunities to use it at different times to support their relationship. We can say, "Remember the time when this work team. . . ." Remembering the data is also important so as to be sure that what we are telling them is based on what we have seen and heard, not on our own biases and distortions. Data-based interventions help to minimize our projecting parts of our own unfinished business (countertransference) onto the present situation (Melnick, 2003).

You have to speak to them in a way that they understand and accept. For example, we have found that our students (and sometimes we ourselves) often use jargon or professional language. Every profession has its own terminology that others cannot understand very well. Some of our favorite overused words are *resistance, contact, aware, energy*, *deep, experiment,* and *love.* It's important to avoid using jargon and technical language with your clients.

Lastly, you have to intervene in a balanced way. You have to address *the interactions between and among people* and not favor one person over another.

(8) Share an Observed Competency with Your Client

When intervening with a work group, you might decide to point out, for example, their high interest in their work, or the fact that they are highly responsive to each other. This is *not a positive reframing.* We are not taking something that we see as negative and finding a way to say it so that it does not deflate them. We are seeing the beauty and the competency in what they are doing, and in how they are doing it. We try always to remember that they *are doing the best they can.*

We have found that most people are clear about

what they don't do well and have no idea about what they do well. Our model says that telling people what they do well, in such a way that they can hear it, is of more value because mentioning the negative gives you nothing else to do, while the positive opens up possibilities. Since they are not aware of what they do well, they often do not focus on it. If they object, we tell them that we will get to the negative in a while—and we do get to it!

When we get interested in our strengths and competencies, we have many more choices as to what to do in the world, and we have a more supportive base for handling the tough things. This allows us to feel stronger. We end up feeling bolder, able to meet the challenges in our lives. The truth is that most of the real troubles in the world are difficult to solve, but we can learn to approach them with optimism and energy. That is what makes it easier to live a good life (Melnick and S. Nevis, 2005).

In *Figure* 7 we describe the first five stages of two interveners following the model as they work with a couple.

Figure 7

Interveners (I) Joining the Client (C) System

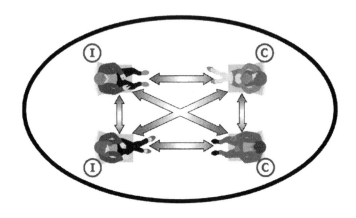

Pulling Back and Observing

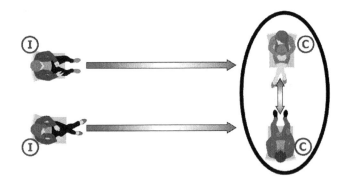

Interrupting

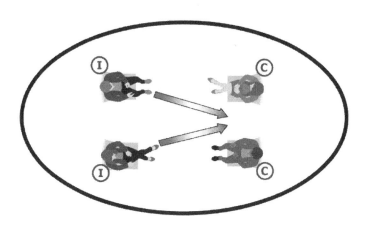

Interveners Consulting

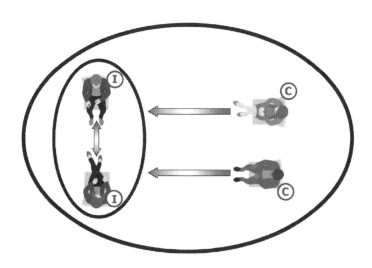

Interveners Giving Feedback

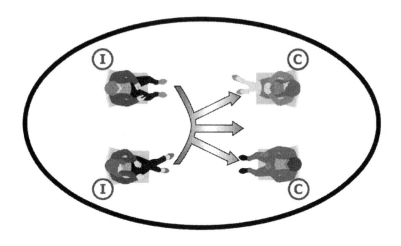

(9) See If What You Told Them Sticks

After you have told them about a competency you have found interesting, look to see if they understand, and if your words matter to them. If they seem confused by what you have said, ask them directly if they understand what you have told them, and if it makes sense to them. If not, you might then describe what you saw (the phenomenological data) to formulate your feedback. If they still seem uncertain or confused, continue to talk to them until you are sure they get it. If they do not, then own your part in confusing them, and tell them that you will sit back again and pay attention to what they are doing.

Acknowledging your role in this missed connection is what we refer to as *selective transparency*. It moves you temporarily into the role of peer and often serves to increase trust on both sides.

Once you are sure they understand your observation, ask them to turn to each other. Sit back again and pay attention to what happens next, to see if what you told them *sticks.* You know it is sticking if they begin to talk with each other about your feedback. If they jump over it and go back to their old conversation in the same way as before, then you know you have had only minimal impact, and it is important to understand why. There could be many reasons. For example:

- You have not spent enough time creating connection and trust.
- The intervention was unbalanced and favored one person or subsystem over another.
- What you said—though accurate—was obvious to them. For example, to tell a sophisticated work group that they are able to disagree with each other would not grab their attention.
- You gave them information before they were psychologically ready to hear it. You did not prepare them well enough or create enough support.
- They were still engaged in the conversation they had been having and did not fully hear what you had to say.
- You did not present what you saw in such a way that it grabbed their interest. Your intervention lacked impact.
- You just missed it. You may have been working your own agenda or your unfinished business.

(10) Interrupt the System, Consult, and Inform the Clients of the Price They Pay

Competent people understand that, because they are good at some things, they are probably not good at others. It is easy just to turn to the old things we do well

237

and neglect the development of new skills and tools. We understand that this is particularly true when we are in trouble. In those moments, we stick to the old habits that had worked in the past—without awareness or choice—rather than trying something different. In doing this we pay a price, for we are not growing and developing.

> **Joe:** *One common pattern we find in organizations is the favoring of either strategy or intimacy. One group I recently began working with spends a lot of time creating strategic plans. If the plan is not working, they create another one. In our work together, they began to realize that what was less developed was their connectedness; what we call their intimacy. They simply did not know how to disagree with each other in a respectful and useful way. But rather than move towards developing this and other intimacy skills, their habit was to continue to fine tune their strategic plan. Once they understood this, they were able to move forward.*

Following your first intervention, which focused on a well-developed competency, you pull back and after consulting with your partner, address the *cost* of doing what they do well over and over again. When working with a "passionate" couple, for example, you might tell them: "Though we admire your high energy, and though there are lots of positives to this way of being together, there are costs." For example, you might ask them if they notice that they often talk at the same time; or although there is a good deal of output, neither one seems to be taking in what the other is saying. Or you might say that there is rarely a pause in their conversation, that they seldom rest to catch their breath, and that they both know how to lean in, but seldom sit back. Here are some examples of common patterns and the costs:

- If they are competent at expressing themselves and have a high degree of *other-directed energy,* then they might have difficulty in turning inward and experiencing hurt, or inner-directed pain and joy.
- If they are good at giving each other space, they might not be so good at *reaching across* and impacting each other.
- If they are creative at talking about many things, they might be less competent at talking about one issue at a time.
- If they are good at being *in balance,* then they might be less competent at focusing on just one or the other.

Interventions addressing strengths are relatively easy to take in when compared to costs and weaknesses. Those that focus on the less developed aspects of relationships are more difficult because they are often out of the clients' awareness or, if the clients are aware, they may have been unsuccessful in changing these patterns. For example, after our intervention, our *passionate* couple might begin to sit back and let in what the other says, but after a while may return to their competency—lots of energy and output and little sitting back and taking in.

Often when we tell our clients the cost of their competency, they begin immediately to try new things. This can lead to a sense of delight regarding what they are learning and doing differently. But habits, especially interactional ones, are hard to change. Frequently, they return quickly to old ways of relating without even noticing the shift back. Sometimes they simply find that doing something new is too difficult. When this happens, we suggest an experiment, what we call a *"Let's Try."*

(11) Interrupt the System Again, Consult, Suggest a "Let's Try"

It is now time to try a different form of intervention that is based on *doing*. It is one thing to talk about doing something different, or to read about it in an instruction manual. It is quite another to practice.

At this point interrupt them once more, ask them to listen to your consult, and then tell them what you have been noticing. You might tell them this: "We have seen some changes in how you interact. While you still each express yourself fully and with passion, you have begun to take turns speaking. But the change isn't sticking. You quickly return to the old pattern." Ask them if they noticed this, and see if they agree with you. If they do, ask them if they would be interested in *trying* something. (And of course, if they haven't noticed, we don't proceed further without a discussion). Some will agree instantly without your needing to say more, but most want to understand what they are accepting. Tell them what you would like them to try and why. So, for example, you might ask our passionate couple if they are willing to alternate talking with the speaker leaning forward, and the listener leaning back. Or you might give them each a pen to converse through writing. Or you might ask each to count to three before responding to a comment. Or you might . . .

Trying is about acting, moving, and doing. There is no right or wrong "Try this." While they are practicing, it is important that you feel free to support them psychologically and emotionally as they are trying the agreed upon task. Are they struggling and need more help, or are they able to do the task easily? Do they need something a little more challenging or complex? Often, they will tell us what will make this experiment interesting and challenging. As mentioned above, we call this shaping "grading" (Zinker, 1977).

At the end, what they try is co-created by your clients and you. As they take more responsibility for their learning, what they find often surprises all of us. After they have completed what they have tried, you then ask them to discuss their experience.

(12) Meaning Making and Ending Well

A good ending gives one a sense of completion. This is true whether it is a piece of music, a good meal, or a life well spent. It allows for energy to ebb as you and your clients reflect on what you just did, and for your experience to become part of your past. Your task is to:

- Reinforce the learning; make space to support closing down as opposed to opening up;
- Encourage the clients to be interested in how they end (For example, you might ask them to tell you what the session or meeting was like and to summarize what they have learned);
- Ask meaning-making questions, such as: What stood out for you? What did you learn? What did you like/dislike? What was hard/easy for you?
- Move out of the experience, broadening your discussion with *small talk.* This helps to transition smoothly back into normal life.

Giving Feedback

At the end of each piece of work, we process the experience as a group with all the participants, first giving feedback to the interveners. We have a specific way of doing this. We focus on the interveners' competence and we look at their skills.

- First, we ask the interveners to give themselves and

241

their partners a specific type of feedback: to discuss what they did well as individuals and as a pair. We are often surprised at how much difficulty our students have in saying something authentically positive about what they did. Sadly, this difficulty continues for many during the entire program.

- We then ask the *couple, family,* or *work team* to also give feedback to the interveners, focusing on how the interventions impacted them.
- We then turn to the observers. They are asked to present their feedback to the interveners in such a way that it is *understandable and impactful.*
- We end each segment with the faculty giving feedback to the interveners about what they did well, and what might be their next developmental steps. Often, at this point, we help our students recognize their difficulties in noticing and talking about their competencies. And, of course, we try to tie our feedback to Gestalt theory and to the Cape Cod Model. It is here in the practicums—not in the lectures—where most of the important learning takes place. Below is a schematic design of the configuration of the individuals in the practicum.

Figure 8

Intervening, Week One

I = Intervener
C = Client
O = Observer

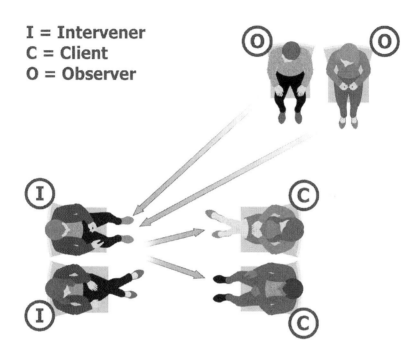

The faculty rotates among these practicum groups throughout the week, rather than being assigned to one. This is done to discourage our students from thinking that there is only *one* way to practice the model. It is our experience that we are enough alike so that trainees are not confused, and different enough so that they get an alternate perspective and emphasis from each of us. This shifting of faculty makes it easy for them to learn different things and eventually develop their own style.

Process Groups

Ongoing process groups take place at the end of each day and are designed to help the participants make sense out of their experience. They are composed in such a way as to maximize heterogeneity. Each process group is facilitated (not lead) by faculty members who work in pairs, with each pair spending a week with a group. Our goal is for us to be available to provide whatever support is needed and to help the day end well. We have changed our roles over the years. Until recently, we would rotate so that the trainees' primary connection would be with each other and not with us. We would usually remain silent, rarely offering up more than a few observations. More recently, we have become more active, focusing primarily on the here and now experience and interactional patterns (Melnick, 1980).

In Closing

Students who participate in the Cape Cod Training Program are immersed in a model that is based on a whole compendium of values, skills, and techniques that can be applied personally and professionally in their lives. And, in addition, they leave knowing how to intervene successfully with an array of groupings that include couples, families, work groups, boards, and other systems. After intensive practice, they are able to assist clients in creating a full cycle with each other that includes an increased awareness of their relational interactions. This involves both the positives and the negatives of their patterns and habits. Our students learn, however, that this awareness is often not enough for new learning to occur. So they support their clients to move to action, to try something different. Last, they help them deconstruct their experience as they digest what they have learned. This represents the meaning-making stage of the Cycle of Experience. At this point, their clients' energy gradually decreases, leading to withdrawal and the opportunity to begin a new cycle.

In this Model, we create a learning community where everyone is open to giving and receiving feedback, to recognizing competencies and developmental opportunities, and to being impacted and changed.

14

CONCLUSION

Sonia*:* *I remember once writing that experience is messy, continuous, disorganized, shapeless, chaotic, and overlapping. We as humans are predisposed to organize our experience into patterns in order to make our way.*

Joe: *That's why I have always appreciated the Cycle of Experience. It gives us an elegant way to organize experience in relation to the situation that we are a part of, with the two coordinates being time and energy.*

Sonia: *That reminds me that we had one more goal that we talked about at the beginning; to present the Cape Cod Model as not just a method for teaching relational change, but as a philosophy and methodology for living in the world.*

Joe: *I remember an experience that was life changing for me. It was over 35 years ago and I was a student in the Cape Cod Training Program. My family, consisting of my wife Gloria, and our children, Spencer, age six, and Alysia, age four, agreed to be a demonstration family. You and Joseph (Zinker) were the interveners. As you began talking to us, Gloria and I described how exhausted we were living far away from relatives and both working full time jobs. We talked about being the children of immigrants who loved us but were unable to support us in some fundamental ways. In response, we both committed ourselves always to be*

	responsive to our children. As we spoke with pride about our values, Joseph and you noticed how our kids were constantly interrupting us, and how we were allowing them to do so.
Sonia:	*Yes, I remember now. After talking to you about the positives and negatives of this value, we suggested that you experiment by continuing to talk to each other even when your children attempted to draw your attention. And within a relatively short time they began playing with each other, and the two of you began to smile.*
Joe:	*That brief experience changed the way we functioned as a family. And, of course, it drew me toward the precursor to the Cape Cod Model and toward working with you.*
Sonia:	*I'm glad it did.*

All important endings involve loss no matter how well done they are. And it is this loss that creates much of the learning embedded in any ending. Is it simply the loss of possibilities or something more complex and hard to define? Is it the loss of imagined dialogue? It seems trite to say something like, "We hope you, the reader, have enjoyed (learned from, been stimulated by, benefited from reading, etc.) this book." What we really hope is that this book has invited you to look at how you live in the world, both personally and professionally. Our wish would be that one or two of our paragraphs caused some small challenge to how you organize yourself and your relationships.

In our introduction, we said that this book was not just about a model of how to teach practitioners to help people change and develop, but how to live well. We also presented a set of core beliefs that we asked you to think about as we described the Cape Cod Model. In closing, we would like to reiterate them. We hope that you will recognize them as embedded in much of what we have presented.

- Awareness offers the opportunity to change. When something becomes a habit, we are no longer aware of what we are doing. For example, most of us are not aware of how we brush our teeth, drive our car, eat our soup, or talk to each other. When we become aware, we notice. Only when we notice do we have a choice between making a change, or doing things as we always have.
- Sometimes awareness can lead to depression and sadness, as when we become aware of pain, or we become aware of wants that cannot be fulfilled.
- Some of us pay attention to thoughts first and others first to emotions. To live well in the world, we have to be able to attend to both. Competency involves an ability to be in touch with both thoughts and emotions and being able to think *and* feel before acting.
- We all carry the past forever within us. The future—including our hopes, wishes, plans, fantasies, and daydreams—also exists. Yet we don't live in the past or the future as much as we would sometimes like. The *now* is all we really have.
- Every experience is composed of many ingredients that shift as a function of the moment and of the situation. It is the situation that is the primary organizer of experience, but most of the time it doesn't feel that way.
- Whenever two or more people are interacting—working together or talking to each other—whatever happens has been crafted by all involved. As simple as it sounds, it is a radical departure from how most of us understand our process.
- Every habit—whether good or bad—was used

initially to solve a problem. Most of our habits continue to be useful. Some, however, are no longer productive, but we continue to use them anyway. For example, many of us are taught to *be respectful,* more specifically, *not* to *interrupt when others are talking.* But if we always wait for a break in the conversation to speak, it might never happen. As a result, we might not express good thoughts or creative solutions that could help solve a problem. If we don't know how to speak up, how will people know what we know?

- The future is always unknown. We do not know what the next second, day, or year will bring. What we call spirituality is how we relate to the unknown. The unknown can scare, excite, confuse, or intimidate us. Some of us rely on hope and faith to support us in facing the uncertain future. We require a special form of competence to deal with the unknown. It consists primarily of the *courage* to sit with uncertainty.

- Resisting can be useful or useless. Competency involves knowing when to say *yes* and when to say *no.* This allows us to know when to act and when to wait, when to try new things and when to stick with the old.

- No one has ever awoken saying, "I am going to mess up my day." We don't plan on making mistakes, forgetting to make the important telephone call, talking too long with a boring person, denting our car, having a horrible meal, losing our keys, or yelling at our children. Most of us are doing the best we can, even when things don't work out as we had expected or hoped.

- Even the best of us messes up often. To turn against ourselves after we err is rarely useful. To experience competency is to know that these things are ordinary, and that the next day will bring new mishaps. And, every once in a while, we have a perfect day.

- Nobody owns the truth. There are many ways to look at phenomena, since we all see things differently. Competent behavior involves a willingness to talk and listen to other people who are different or who have different points of view.[37]

- Power is neither good nor bad, nor does it exist solely within individuals. Power exists *between* people, groups, and even nations. At its core, power is a relationship—not an attribute. A powerful person, group, or nation is skilled at influencing and open to being influenced. Some people are given power by their position, i.e., a parent or an employer, and they can use it for good or for ill.

- Most of our relationships contain some form of hierarchy, whether implied or explicit. In nearly all relationships there are differences in levels of knowledge or skill, and sometimes people are put in charge of others as leaders. Hierarchy needs to be acknowledged and respected, and the rules for clear communication understood by all. The health of a hierarchical system, such as a family or nation, depends on the relational competence of those in the hierarchy.

- We are always having impact, both good and bad, depending on how we present ourselves to others. We call our self-presentation *presence*. Becoming aware of our presence leads to acting with intention. Whether we are modeling a behavior, bringing a missing aspect to the process, choosing to remain silent, or joining with the group, we are always having an influence.

- Maturity, in part, involves creating lives that are filled

---

[37] There is much research that supports this notion. Even the legal system is questioning the validity of eye-witnesses.

with possibilities. We are able to move towards things that have potential, to feel regret when things don't turn out as expected, and to move on, having learned from the experience.

- And most important, growth and development come from our movement toward what is different from the way we are.

APPENDIX A

GESTALT CORE CONCEPTS

Awareness
Gestalt believes that an individual or system is performing at its optimum based on its current awareness. At the center of the Gestalt perspective is the concept of awareness. If we believe in the potential of an individual and their self-responsibility, then the core concept to effecting change in the individual is through the expansion of their awareness. By raising awareness, we enable the individual or the organization to maintain responsibility and make the changes that are most appropriate and in their interests.

Boundary
The point (contact) at which the "me" and the "not me" is made or broken. It is also the point of intention.

Contact
Contact is the term used to define the nature and qualities of human interaction. Individuals are always in contact with their environment and often with other people. The extent to which individuals are aware, present, and engaged reflects their level of contact. We often experience a "connection" with another person or have "good conversations" where people feel that the communication is honest and real. People who are able to make connections, communicate effectively, and relate well to others, or have high "emotional intelligence," are people who are able to make contact with others. In Gestalt work, we help people to improve their ability to make contact with others and to have a greater impact on their lives. We do this by helping

others to develop the skills for connecting, as well as by teaching people to identify and remove the barriers to good contact.

Cycle of Experience
Gestalt is focused on building skill in the process of perceiving, deciding, acting, learning, and improving. This process is called the Cycle of Experience. The Cycle of Experience describes an interactive cycle that moves from awareness through contact, action, integration, and closure, providing both a framework and a template to observe for competence and for areas that need further development.

Experiments
Gestalt practice is distinct because it moves toward action and away from "talking about," and for this reason it is considered an applied approach. Through trying new ways of doing things, we support the individual's direct experience of something new, instead of merely talking about the possibility of something new.

Figure/Ground
Some things are more important than others, and what we choose to arrest our gaze upon shapes the experience of our life. How we perceive the information available to us, and how we choose what action we will take, depends on the full amount of information available (ground). This includes situational data, as well as data about our physical and emotional reaction and experience. From that we make choices about what we will focus on (figure) above anything else. The greater the ground work, the better the figure. Raising awareness is often about adding information to the ground before a person, group, or organization chooses to focus on a figure.

Intention

When individuals or organizations operate without awareness, they operate without intention. Unexpected and disappointing consequences often emerge when decisions and actions are taken without intention. As an individual or organization becomes more aware, they are better able to make decisions and take actions from a point of clear intention. This often results in an individual's or organization's needs being met more fully. An important corollary to raising awareness is helping individuals and organizations develop clarity around their intentions.

Level of System

Things are happening everywhere, all the time. An individual experiences anxiety, two people have an argument, a group decides to take action, or an organization experiences a trauma. When working with a system, we need to increase our awareness of what is happening and at what level, and determine how we want to impact the system and at what level. Do we help by talking to a senior executive in a key function, or with a group of field people? Do we need to have broad communication across a group, or will a personal discussion with someone make a difference? Understanding how people and organizations work allows us to see how best to influence and impact their success.

Multiple Realities

We emphasize the concept of multiple realities. We acknowledge that we each bring our unique experience and perception to the situation, and that there are always multiple ways of making meaning out of a given moment—all of which are real to the individual. We place great emphasis on teaching people how to manage differences.

Optimistic Stance
Gestalt takes a realistic view of the present and an optimistic view of the possible. We prefer to work in the development of the potential within an individual or system rather than correcting them.

Polarities
Polarities are the natural process of opposites: Sad/Happy, Hot/Cold, Generous/Stingy. There is a tendency to move to one side and call it a good thing, and to call the other side bad. Our stance is that both ends of every polarity are important, depending on the circumstance. Growth and development is the stretching that incorporates the whole spectrum.

Presence
Who we are as individuals and how we present ourselves to others is at the core of our presence. In Gestalt practice, we believe that an individual's presence has the ability to impact another person, group, or organization. Becoming increasingly aware of our presence, and acting with intention on how we use our presence, is a discipline of Gestalt work. Whether we are modeling a behavior, bringing a missing presence, or joining existing energy, we are always having an impact.

Resistance
It is a force that slows or stops movement. It is a natural and expected part of change. Understanding the resistance and leaning into it releases energy to move forward. It is a paradox.

Self-Responsibility
Gestalt practice firmly advocates that the individual or

system has responsibility for itself. Only by taking responsibility for our decisions and actions are we able to change and improve our experience and interaction in the world. It is up to the individual or the system to change itself.

Strategic and Intimate Systems©
Behaviors that create trust and safety, and balancing interactions to produce a seamless braid, result in the best possible outcome.

Theory of Change
Only an individual, group, or organization can change itself. The challenge of the Gestalt practitioner (coach, consultant, clinician) is to raise the awareness of the individual, group, or organization so that it decides to change itself. The paradox is that the more a system attempts to be what it is not, the more it remains the same. Conversely, when people identify with their current experience, the conditions of wholeness and growth support change.

Unit of Work
Each person, group, or organization has any number of obligations, responsibilities, expectations, activities, tasks, and other "to-dos." Each of these is at various stages of starting and completion. In Gestalt practice, the process of getting work done requires clarity around what it is that is being done and the stage of the Cycle of Experience in which we are working. Being explicit about the boundary and stage of work that is to be completed is referred to as a "unit of work." Being clear on a unit of work and completing the unit with effective closure is an important aspect of the Gestalt approach.

Well Developed/Less Developed©
GISC teaches the concepts of "well developed" and

"less developed" to describe how people tend to lean to one end of the polarity and call it good, while calling the other end of the polarity bad. At times, one may use the well-developed because it is an automatic way of being. Overuse of any behavior narrows one's choices. Understanding Well Developed/Less Developed© theory allows for the opening of more possibilities.

APPENDIX B

A SAMPLING OF RECENT BOOKS THAT EXPAND GESTALT THEORY

Groups

Cole, P., & Reese, D. (2018). *New directions in Gestalt group therapy. Relational ground, authentic self.* New York: Routledge.

Feder, B. & Frew, J., Eds. (2008). *Beyond the Hot Seat Revisited.* New Orleans: The Gestalt Institute Press.

Gaffney, S. (2013). *Groups, Teams and Groupwork Revisited.* Australia: Ravenwood.

Leadership

Barber, P. (2012). *A reflective guide to facilitating change in groups and teams – A Gestalt approach to mindfulness.* Oxford: Libri Press.

Congram, S., Mayes, R., & Musselbrook, M. (2015). *Engendering balance: A fresh approach to leadership.* Dolgarren, St Weonards: Engendering Balance Publishing.

Dvergsdal, D., (2014). *Expanding your leadership: A journey towards building character.* Oslo: Abstrat forlag AS.

Elsner, R. & Farrands, B. (2012). *Leadership transitions: How business leaders take charge in new roles.* London: Kogan Page.

Organizations

Chidiac, M.-A. (In Press). *Relational organizational Gestalt: An emergent approach to organizational development.* London: Karnac.

Gross, T., (2011). *Mobilizing commitment.* USA: Ex Libris.

Hardaway, N. (2013). *The awareness paradigm. New* York: Merrimack Media.

APPENDIX C

UNFINISHED BUSINESS AND DISTORTIONS (COUNTERTRANSFERENCE ISSUES) WHEN WORKING WITH OR IN AN ORGANIZATION

- There are perforce more countertransference possibilities in organization work than in individual (coaching) or two-person system work.
- You, as interveners, must attend to how your roles in your family of origin impact your work in organizations (e.g., values, behaviors, and attitudes).
- Attend to your capacity for compassion vis-à-vis how people think and behave in other families/organizations. This requires that you learn to understand (enjoy) the "goodness" of both sides of polarities.
- To work with co-consultants/coaches is valuable, because they might see and respond to what may be invisible to you.
- Watch out for projecting the experience of your organization onto new situations; for example, "I've been on many boards, and this is what we did in a similar situation. . . ."
- Pay attention to your preference for what constitutes a "good" outcome.
- Pay attention to your preference or greater liking for one level of system over another (individual, dyad, group, or system as a whole).
- Be aware of your preference for different hierarchical positions (e.g., leaders, managers, or support staff)
- Pay particular attention to people you experience as being scapegoated.

REFERENCES

Achor, S. (2010). *The happiness advantage: The seven principles of positive psychology that fuel success and performance at work.* New York: Crown Publishing Group.

Allen, W. & Brickman, M. (1977). Annie Hall.

Alter, A. (2017). *Irresistible: The rise of addictive technology and the business of keeping us hooked.* New York: Penguin.

Beisser, A. (1970). The paradoxical theory of change. In J. Fagan & I. Shepherd, I. (Eds.), *Gestalt therapy now: Theory, techniques, and applications* (pp. 77-80). Palo Alto, CA: Science & Behavior Books.

Bohm, D., & Nichol, L. (2004). *On dialogue.* New York: Routledge.

Buber, M. (1937). *I and thou.* Edinburgh: T & T Clark.

Chidiac, M. A., & Denham-Vaughan, S. (2007). The process of presence: Energetic availability and fluid responsiveness, *British Gestalt Journal, 16*(1), 9-19.

Chidiac, M. A., & Denham-Vaughan, S. (2018). Presence for everyone: A Dialogue. *Gestalt Review, 22* (1), 35-49.

Clemmens, M. C. (1997). *Getting beyond sobriety: Clinical approaches to long-term recovery.* New York: Routledge.

Cuddy, A., Kuhut, M., & Noffinger, J. (2013, July/August). Connect then lead. *Harvard Business Review.*

Damasio, A. (1994). *Descartes' error.* New York: Avon.

Duhigg, C. (2014). *The power of habit.* New York: Random House.

Fisher, M. (2017a). (Gestalt) pathways of dissemination, Part I: Origins. *Gestalt Review*, 21(1), 7-22.

Fisher, M. (2017b). (Gestalt) pathways of dissemination, Part II: The hub of the human potential movement. *Gestalt Review*, 21(2), 103-122.

Fisher, M. (2017c). (Gestalt) pathways of dissemination, Part

III: The media firestorm. *Gestalt Review, 21*(3), 200-220.

Fischer, S. (2011) "In search of good form": The aesthetic of contactful writing. *Gestalt Review, 15*(3), 219-223.

Frank, R. (2001). *Body of awareness: A somatic and developmental approach to psychotherapy.* Cambridge, MA: Gestalt Press.

Heath, C., & Heath, D. (2007). *Made to stick: Why some ideas survive and others die.* New York: Random House.

Holman, P., & Devane, T. (Eds.) (1999). *The change handbook: Group methods for shaping the future.* San Francisco: Berrett-Koehler Publishers.

Isaacs, W. (1999). *Dialogue: The art of thinking together.* New York: Doubleday.

Kabat-Zinn, J. (1994). *Wherever you go there you are.* New York: Hyperion.

Kepner, J. (1987). *Body process: A Gestalt approach to working with the body in psychotherapy.* New York: GIC Press.

Lee, R. G., & Wheeler, G. (1997). *The voice of shame: Silence and connection in psychotherapy.* Hillsdale, NJ: The Analytic Press.

Levine, P. A. (1997). *Waking the tiger: Healing trauma.* Berkeley: North Atlantic Books.

Maine Sunday Telegram (Dec. 2013). U.S. has become a nation of distrusters. Portland, Maine.

Mauer, R. (2010). *Beyond the wall of resistance.* Austin, Texas: Bard Press.

McConville, M. (1995). *Adolescence: Psychotherapy and the emergent self.* San Francisco: Jossey-Bass.

Melnick, J. (1980a). Gestalt group process therapy. *The Gestalt Journal, 3(*2), 86-96.

Melnick, J. (1980b). The use of therapist imposed structure in Gestalt therapy. *The Gestalt Journal, 3,* 4-20. (Reprinted1985). In W. Walsh (Ed.), *Childhood and adolescence* (pp. 148-164). Berkeley: McCutchen.

Melnick, J. (2003). Countertransference and the Gestalt

approach. *British Gestalt Journal, 12*(1), 40-48.

Melnick, J. (2011). Sonia March Nevis: The reluctant writer. *Gestalt Review, 15*(1), 79-91.

Melnick, J., & Nevis, E. (Eds.) (2012). *Mending the world: Social healing interventions by Gestalt practitioners worldwide.* New York: Routledge (Taylor, & Francis).

Melnick, J., & Nevis, S. (1987). Power, choice and surprise. *The Gestalt Journal, 9,* 43-51.

Melnick, J. & Nevis, S. (1997). Diagnosing in the here and now: The experience cycle and DSM-IV. *British Gestalt Journal, 6*(2), 97-106.

Melnick, J. & Nevis, S. (1998). Intimacy and power in long-term relationships. *Australian Gestalt Journal, 2*(2), 39-52.

Melnick, J., & Nevis, S. (2003). Creativity in long-term intimate relationships. In M. Spagnuolo Lobb & N. Amendt-Lyon (Eds.), *Creative license: The art of Gestalt therapy* (pp. 227-238). Wien, Austria: Springer-Verlag.

Melnick, J., & Nevis, S. (2005). The willing suspension of disbelief: Optimism. *Gestalt Review,* 9(1), 10-26.

Melnick, J., & Nevis, S. (2006a). Being with another: The development and maintenance of intimacy. *Gestalt Journal of Australia and New Zealand, 2*(2), 29-41.

Melnick, J., & Nevis, S. (2006b). Love and commitment in the 21st century. *British Gestalt Journal, 15*(2), 28-35.

Melnick, J., & Nevis, S. (2010). Contempt. *Gestalt Review, 14*(3), 215-231.

Melnick, J., & Nevis, S. (2016). Optimism. *Gestalt Review,* 21(3), 191-199.

Melnick, J., Nevis, S., & Melnick, G. (1995). Living with desire: An essay. *British Gestalt Journal, 4,* 31-40.

Melnick, J. & Roos, S. (2007). The myth of closure. *Gestalt Review, 11*(2), 90-107.

Merry, U., & Brown, G. (1987). *The neurotic behavior of organizations.* Cleveland: Gestalt Institute of Cleveland Press.

Mortola, P., Hiton, H., & Grant, S. (2007). *BAM! Boys advocacy and mentoring: A leader's guide to facilitating strengths-based groups for boys: Helping boys make better contact by making better contact with them.* New York: Routledge.

Neff, K. (2011). *Self-compassion: Stop beating yourself up and leave insecurity behind.* New York: HarperCollins.

Nevis, E. (1987). *Organizational consulting: A Gestalt approach.* New York: Gardner Press.

Nevis, E. (Ed.). (1992). *Gestalt therapy: Perspectives and applications.* New York: Gardner Press.

Nevis, E. (2009). Commentary II: The cycle of experience recycled: Then, now. . . next? *Gestalt Review, 13*(1), 37-41.

Nevis, E., Melnick, J., & Nevis, S. (2008). Organizational change through powerful micro-level interventions: The Cape Cod Model. *OD Practitioner, 3(40), 4-8.

Nevis, E., Nevis, S. M., & Zinker, J. (1986). Intimacy and play in long-term relationship. *Center for the Study of Intimate Systems News,* 2 (3), 1-4.

Papernow, P. (1993). *Becoming a stepfamily: Patterns of development in remarried families.* Cambridge, MA: Gestalt Press.

Parker-Pope, T. (2011). Go easy on yourself, a new wave of research urges. *New York Times Wellness Blog.* http://well.blogs.nytimes.com/2011/02/28/go-easy-on-yourself-a-new-wave-of-research-urges /?_r=0

Parlett, M. (1992). Reflections on field theory. *British Gestalt Journal, 1*(2), 69-81.

Perls, F. (1969). *Gestalt therapy verbatim.* Lafayette, CA: Real People Press.

Perls F., Hefferline, R., & Goodman, P. (1951). *Gestalt therapy: Excitement and growth in the human personality* . New York: Julian Press.

Peterson, C. (2000). The future of optimism. *American Psychologist, 55*(1), 44-55.

Pfeiffer, J. W. & Jones, J. E. (1975). *Instrumentation in human relations training: A guide to ninety-two instruments with wide application to the behavioral sciences.* San Diego: University Associates Publishers and Consultants.

Polster, E. & Polster, M. (1973). *Gestalt therapy integrated: Contours of theory and practice.* New York: Brunner/Mazel.

Rilke, R. M. (1934). *Letters to a young poet* (4th letter, dated July 16, 1903), M. D. Herter Norton (trans.). New York: W. W. Norton, pp. 33-34.

Robine, J-M. (2015). *Social change begins with two.* Milan, Italy: Instituto di Gestalt HCC.

Rosenberg, M. (2012). *Living nonviolent communication: Practical tools to connect and communicate skillfully in every situation.* Boulder, CO: Sounds True.

Roubal, J. (2009). Experiment: A creative phenomenon of the field, *Gestalt Review, 13*(3), 263-276.

Roubal, J., Brownell, P., Francesetti, G., Melnick, J., & Zeleskov-Djoric, J. (Eds.) (2016). *Towards a research tradition in Gestalt therapy.* Newcastle upon Tyne, UK: Cambridge Scholars Publishing.

Seligman, M. E. P. (1991). *Learned optimism.* New York: Knopf.

Staemmler, F-M. (2015). The many voices of the self. *British Gestalt Journal 24*(2), 5-13.

Stone, D., & Heen, S. (2015). *Thanks for the feedback: The science and art of receiving feedback well.* New York: Penguin.

Stone, D. and Patton, B. (2010). *Difficult conversations: How to discuss what matters most.* New York: Penguin Books.

Strossel, S. (2013). *My age of anxiety: Fear, dread, and the search for peace of mind.* New York: Vintage.

Taylor, M. (2013). On safe ground: Using sensorimotor approaches in trauma. *British Gestalt Journal, 22*(2), 5-13.

Weisel, E. (1986). Interview with U.S. Media.

Weir, K. (2011). Golden rule redux. *Monitor on Psychology*, (July/August), 42(7), 12-14.

Wheeler, G. (1991). *Gestalt reconsidered, a new approach to contact and resistance* (2nd ed.). Cambridge, MA: The Gestalt Institute of Cleveland.

Wheeler, G., & Axellson, L. (2015). *Gestalt therapy*. Washington, D.C.: American Psychological Association.

Wheeler, G., & Backman, S. (1994) (Eds.). *On intimate ground*. San Francisco: Jossey-Bass.

Wicklund, R., & Gollwitzer, P. (1981). Symbolic self-completion, attempted influence, and self-deprecation. *Basic and Applied Social Psychology*, 2(2), 89-114.

Wiseman, R. (2007). *Quirkology*. London: Pan Macmillan.

Wollants, G. (2012). *Gestalt therapy: Therapy of the situation*. London: Sage.

Yankelovich, D. (2001). *The magic of dialogue: Transforming conflict into cooperation*. New York: Touchstone.

Zinker, J. (1977). *Creative process in Gestalt therapy*. New York: Brunner/Mazel.

Made in the USA
Lexington, KY
13 June 2019